The
WRATH
of
IRENE

*Vermont's Imperfect
Stom of 2011*

The
Public
Press

The
WRATH
of
IRENE

*Vermont's Imperfect
Storm of 2011*

M. Dickey Drysdale
Editor, The Herald of Randolph
with contributions from Staff and Friends

Stephen Morris and Sandy Levesque, Co-Editors

The Public Press

Co-edited by Stephen Morris and Sandy Levesque

Cover photos by:
Background Water, Bob Eddy
White River Under Construction, Tim Calabro

Cover and text design by Nancy Cassidy

Our Pledge

We have selected the Central Vermont Community Action Council to be the beneficiaries of a charitable donation from the revenues of this book. This donation will grow the longer the book stays in print and the more copies that are sold.

We've selection CVCAC because the territory they serve closely overlaps with the White River watershed. Although they are not specifically related to the damages caused by Irene, they are focused on combating poverty. As is stated on their website (cvcac.org): "Poverty impacts everyone – young and old, men and women, families and individuals. When one person or family is helped out of poverty, we strengthen our entire community. It takes action, people working together to make a difference."

That's a lesson we learned from Irene, and one we hope to never forget.

CONTENTS

President Calvin Coolidge

The most famous words ever written about Vermont—and the most moving—were spoken by U. S. President Calvin Coolidge at Bennington on September 21, 1928. Ten months after the devastating 1927 flood, Coolidge was touring the state, making note of the amazing recovery. He discovered the same resiliency Vermonters and others are now discovering after the flood occasioned by Hurricane Irene in August 2011.

"It is gratifying to note the splendid recovery from the great catastrophe which overtook the state nearly a year ago. Transportation has been restored. The railroads are in a better condition than before. The highways are open to traffic for those who wish to travel by automobile."

Despite his later reputation as "Silent Cal," Coolidge was considered a dynamic public speaker in his many campaigns for office in Massachusetts, and he was one of the best writers of all American presidents (second only to Lincoln, according to Vermont historian Howard Coffin). The words he delivered in 1928 have lived in Vermonters' hearts ever since.

My Fellow Vermonters ...

Vermont is a state I love. I could not look upon the peaks of Ascutney, Killington, Mansfield, and Equinox, without being moved in a way that no other scene could move me. It was here that I first saw the light of day; here I received my bride, here my dead lie pillowed on the loving breast of our eternal hills.

I love Vermont because of her hills and valleys, her scenery and invigorating climate, but most of all because of her indomitable people. They are a race of pioneers who have almost beggared themselves to serve others.

If the spirit of liberty should vanish in other parts of the Union, and support of our institutions should languish, it could all be replenished from the generous store held by the people of this brave little state of Vermont.

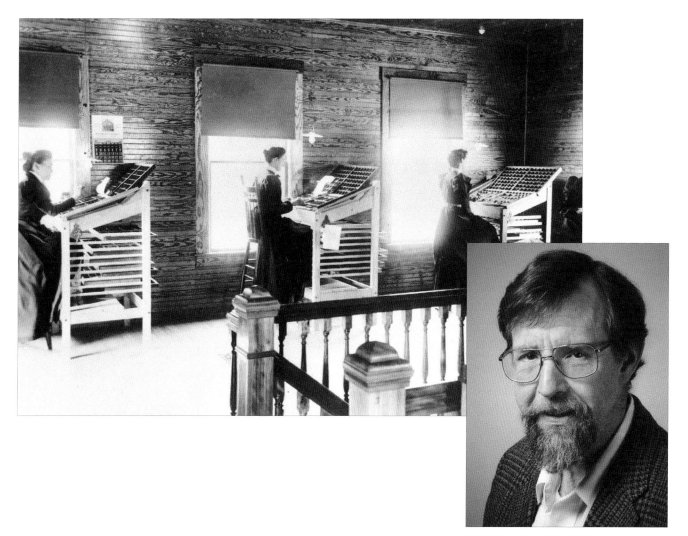

M. Dickey Drysdale, Editor
The Herald of Randolph

PREFACE
M. Dickey Drysdale

J ust months after the Great Flood of 1927, which inspired Calvin Coolidge's immortal tribute to Vermont, *The White River Valley Herald* published "Floodtide of 1927." The 182-page book was spearheaded by Luther B. Johnson, the estimable publisher of *The Herald*, now known as *The Herald of Randolph*. "Floodtide" concentrated on the damage wreaked in the White River Valley watershed.

L. B. Johnson followed that book with two more. "Vermont in Floodtime" told the story from a state-wide perspective, and "The Challenge" dealt with the destruction of the White River Valley " Peavine" Railroad between Bethel and Rochester.

As children, we devoured those books. Both in their shocking photographs and in their vivid writing, they made the flood come alive for us, insuring that succeeding generations would appreciate details— terrible and heroic alike—of Vermont's greatest natural calamity.

The Herald of Randolph staff

So when Stephen Morris of The Public Press approached *The Herald*, a month after the Flood of Irene, with a proposal for a book, we enthusiastically agreed. This flood uncannily resembled the earlier one. It descended upon us as the result of a single torrential rainstorm that followed weeks of wet weather that saturated the ground and was particularly destructive in the White River watershed. Like "Floodtime," our book would focus on the White River Valley. It could tell personal stories of harrowing escape, as well as a deeper, wider story about how hundreds of people stranded in villages or tiny valleys, came together to support each other, plan together, and work like beavers to get the needed work done. We already had the material—stories and photos published in *The Herald* during the months after the flood.

A full "history" of the Flood of Irene will remain for others to write, in due time. But in this volume, through the stories and vivid photography, we hope to bring to folks outside our valley and to future generations a compelling representation of what it was like to witness the ferocity of Irene and the challenges met by Vermonters after she went on her destructive way.

Thanks to our own staff members—especially Martha Slater, who was stranded in Rochester for two weeks—and to our intrepid photographers who followed the trail of destruction wherever it led.

Thanks, too, for those readers—and even strangers—who spontaneously contributed hair-raising accounts, heart-warming tales, and scores of photographs to allow us to document this disaster in a personal, human way, both in our newspaper and in this book.

Finally, thanks are due to Stephen Morris and Sandy Levesque of The Public Press, who came up with the idea of this publication and had the expertise and energy to bring it to reality.

FOREWORD
The Boss Takes a Vacation

M Dickey Drysdale has been publishing The Herald since his father handed it over to him in 1971. Not many in town can remember a time when the local paper did not have a Drysdale sitting at the battle-scarred rolltop desk that is the editor's humble throne.

The boss doesn't take many vacations, because the news doesn't take many vacations. On the rare occasions he does, I sometimes get the call to pinch hit. This means for a week I get to "ride the roll top".

It's always a fun time for me. The veteran staff, some of whom have been there since Gutenberg invented the printing press, are politely tolerant and deferential. They put up with my stupid questions (how do you turn on this computer?). Some even pretend to consult me when making decisions on what goes in The Herald.

The boss asked if I could stand in for him the week of August 29 while he and his wife attended a hiking retreat on Mt. Desert Island on the coast of Maine. Sure!

The week officially starts on the preceding Thursday when the editorial staff previews the hot stories, assigns follow-ups, and hands out reporting and writing gigs. The headline story of the previous week was the earthquake that gently shook Vermont. Not quite a natural disaster, but a natural phenomenon that warranted page one.

The assignments are parceled out, followed by the obligatory small talk. Someone asks the Boss what he is doing for vacation and he tells them about hiking on Mt. Desert Island where they will be camping in tents.

"Uh, you might want to bring some rain gear," said Sandy Vondrasek, his associate editor.

"Why's that?"

"Hurricane Irene," says Martha Slater, the paper's copy editor. "It's supposed to bring heavy rains on Sunday."

MD shrugs. Mentally, so do I. So did everyone in Vermont. Hurricanes don't threaten us. We scoff at hurricanes, as we do at earthquakes, tornadoes, and tsunamis. We're a little afraid of ice dams ... and mud, of course, but we can handle just about everything else nature can throw at us.

So editorial assignments are completed. I have a roster of hardball journalism stories that would bring lesser reporters to their knees, including a report on the anniversary of the Boy Scouts, a look at the Barnard General Store installing WiFi, and a profile of an apple farm in Vershire. Someone is given the task of following up on the previous week's earthquake, but no one is assigned to cover Hurricane Irene. At the end of the meeting we wish The Boss safe travel and joke about him forgetting his rain slicker.

On Friday, Michael Bloomberg, mayor of New York, notches up the Irene alert when he orders the city to be evacuated and closes down the public transportation system. But there's a political element here. He had been criticized for under-reacting the previous winter when the city was slammed by a snowstorm just after Christmas, and seems to be going to great lengths to make sure that experience is not repeated. The forecast for Vermont is for high winds and rain, but hurricanes always lose their teeth when they make it this far inland. No one seems worried.

On Saturday I am surprised to learn via Facebook post that the Drysdales have canceled their trip to Maine. (Facebook, along with the branches of

> *As Vermonters, we scoff at hurricanes, as we do at earthquakes, tornadoes, and tsunamis.*

the White River watershed, becomes one of the surprising characters in this book.) I email Dick, expressing my sympathy and volunteering that maybe *The Herald* does not need a substitute editor if the real one is available. He responds that it was the campground that had canceled their week. As far as he is concerned, he is still on vacation and only the venue has changed. He and Marjie will be spending the week visiting Vermont's beautiful state parks. He might check in at the office, but otherwise is "outtahere."

I arrive at the office Monday morning bright-eyed, bushy-tailed, tankard of coffee in hand, and armed with my personal storm vignettes, but unprepared for the drama taking place in the creaky offices of The Herald.

News sprays like a fire hose in a newspaper office. Dick is at his desk, trying to sort it all out. The next two days are a blur of rumors, dramatic reports, blind alleys, heroic actions, and misinformation. We instantly get busy trying to sort out the fact from fiction, to determine what is, in fact, news. The task is made all the more difficult due to some staffers living in those communities that are isolated from both the world and the twenty-first century. It is controlled chaos.

Most everywhere is without electricity and phone service. Amazingly, downtown Randolph is largely spared any disruption. The dramatic and complex story of Tropical Storm Irene unfolds over the next hours, but then keeps unfolding in the following days and weeks. As the only person in the office with no defined role, I become the official repository for things that no one else knows what to do with. I interview a town manager who admits to being bewildered and overwhelmed, yet who is composed enough to return a call to the local newspaper. I take a call from a near hysterical lady from the devastated Stony Brook community who provides first-hand reports of

houses washed away by raging waters, but who refuses to give her name due to fears of attracting looters. I talk to a fish hatchery supervisor who is in shock from the loss of 90,000 trout that he had spent the last two years raising. I follow up on a report of a dairy farmer who watched part of his herd float down the White River. Amazingly, he answers the phone in his barn, and tells me that in addition to his livestock losses, he has lost his home, and much of his equipment. And what was he doing while talking to me?

"Milkin'," he says without missing a beat. Apparently, the cows were not impressed by the drama of the storm.

Nor do they affect newspaper deadlines. Everyone is on information overload, but there is still a paper to get out. *The Times-Argus*, we learn, can't make it from printer to customer, due to roads being out. *The Vermont Standard*, published continuously for the last 158 years, loses their offices to the Ottauquechee River, yet publisher Phil Camp vows to publish on schedule.

There's a rare moment of quiet on Wednesday morning, publication day. I look up from my makeshift desk (another roll top that I commandeered from Martha Slater, a stranded Rochester resident) and make eye contact with Dick, whose vacation has now been officially blasted to smithereens. We've shared an important moment in Vermont history.

With this project—Irene, the Story—we're reliving it with the benefit of per-spective. While the pain of this disaster will be felt for many years to come, it is matched by tales of inspiration, re-birth, and the human spirit that are also parts of this fascinating and multi-hued story. Irene, the storm, was history by Monday morning, but Irene, the Story, will continue to evolve.

Stephen Morris
Gilead Brook Road
December, 2011

The White River Watershed

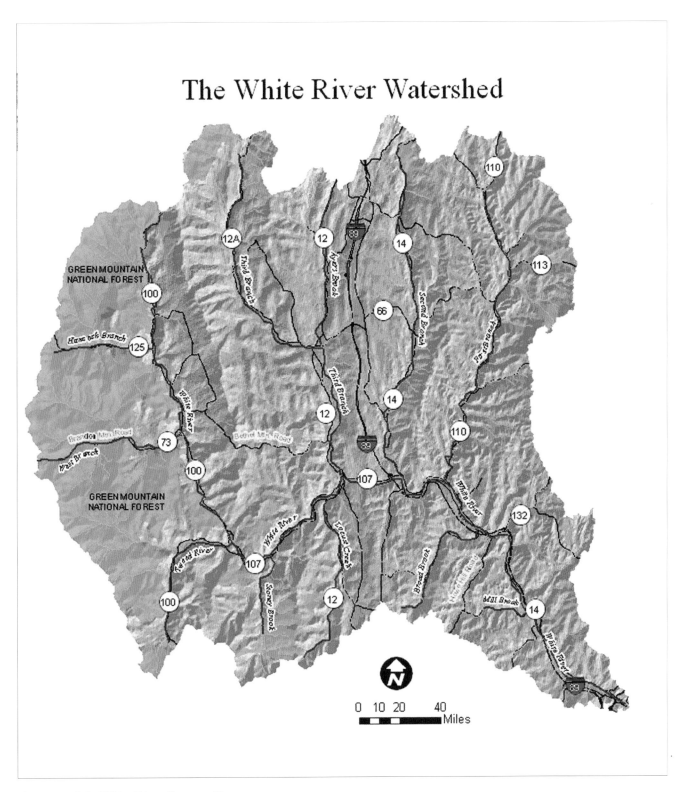

Courtesy of the White River Partnership

INTRODUCTION:
A Cast of Characters

Before there were roads, before there were bridges, before there were buildings, before there were people, there were the mountains and the rivers. This is the story of a time and place when the mountains and rivers behaved very badly, at least from the perspective of those people settled there. It is the story of Tropical Storm Irene's impact on the White River watershed in 2011.

As much as possible, we're telling the story from west to east, and north to south, as the waters flow. But stories, not unlike streams, do not always flow in straight lines.

We asked the White River Partnership, a community-based, nonprofit organization bringing together people and local communities to improve the long-term health of the White River and its watershed in central Vermont, to help us define "watershed":

A watershed is an area of land where all of the rain, snowmelt, and water flowing downhill drain into the same body of water – a river, stream, or lake. Water slides down the sides of the area from the highest point to the bottom of the watershed, like a basin filling with water. On its way, the water travels over the land – across fields, forests, back yards, streets and roads, or seeps into the soil and travels underground (becoming groundwater).

Here are a few facts about our watershed that we learned from the White River Partnership:

There are four major watersheds in the State of Vermont: the Connecticut River watershed (of which the White River watershed is part), the Lake Champlain watershed, the St. Lawrence watershed, and the Hudson River watershed.

The White River watershed encompasses 710 square miles, draining portions of Addison, Orange, Rutland, Washington and Windsor Counties, including 50,000 acres of the Green Mountain National Forest.

The main stem of the White River is one of the last free-flowing rivers in the State of Vermont. As the longest un-dammed tributary to the Connecticut River, which is an American Heritage River, the White River is critical to the Connecticut River Atlantic Salmon Restoration Program – a federal program aimed at revitalizing Atlantic salmon populations.

The White originates in the town of Ripton on the slopes of Battell Mountain, then flows southerly and easterly before merging with the Connecticut River in Hartford. Another source describes the river as starting in Skylight Pond, south of Bread Loaf Mountain near the crest of the Green Mountains.

The 56-mile main stem of the White River has 5 major tributaries: the First Branch, the Second Branch, the Third Branch, the West Branch, and the Tweed River. The tributaries took on widely varying roles in the drama called Irene.

The main stem of the White flows east to the town of Granville, where it receives the outflow from the southern portion of Granville Notch. The river then turns south, running alongside famed Vermont Route 100, flowing through the towns of Hancock and Rochester. Where Route 100 is joined by Route 73, the White is joined by the West Branch, draining the Brandon Mountain basin, including Corporation Brook.

The Tweed River is usually a playful stream that starts on Killington Mountain, then flows south paralleling Route 100 through the town of Pittsfield with its white houses surrounding a picture-perfect Vermont village green. The Tweed has lent its name to both a tubing company and a music festival. It joins up with the White in Stockbridge. It is the second main tributary of the White.

From Stockbridge, the main stem turns northeast and parallels Vermont Route 107, treating travelers to colorful views along a portion of the road nicknamed "Refrigerator Flats." Tubers, swimmers, bridge divers, fly fishermen, and kayakers are common sights. One local resident described it as Vermont's most "used" river (that's not "used" as in "used car," but rather used for recreation, sustenance, and feeding the soul).

In Bethel, at Peavine Park, the White joins forces with its most prominent tributary (in terms of water flow), the Third Branch. This starts as a rivulet called Flint Brook in the hills above Roxbury then is swelled by a series of lively brooks as it makes its way down Route 12A towards Randolph.

First Riford, then Thayer Brook, join the flow. Ayers Brook, which drains the Route 12 basin from the Brookfield Gulf on south, joins the Third Branch just below the tenth green on Montague Golf Course.

South of town the Third Branch receives the waters of two major streams, first Gilead Brook, then Camp Brook before plunging over the dam that still provides electric power for one of Vermont's oldest operating businesses, Bethel Mills.

The Second Branch originates in the Williamstown Gulf and parallels Route 14 before joining the White in Royalton. The First Branch begins in Washington and follows Route 110 through the shire town of Chelsea, then Tunbridge before joining the main river in South Royalton, just across from the Vermont Law School.

Interestingly, the First and Second Branches were relegated to relatively minor parts in the Irene drama, while lesser streams—Stony Brook, Camp Brook, Riford Brook, Thayer Brook, Locust Creek, Jail Brook, and Gilead Brook—stepped into lead roles.

Various enterprises, organizations, and other entities also became characters in Irene, the drama. The watershed is home to two fish hatcheries that couldn't be more different. Tiny Flint Brook provides the pristine water for the picturesque Roxbury fish hatchery, built in 1891 and now on the National Registry of Historical Sites.

The ponds of the fish hatchery are arranged in a park-like setting where the eggs are incubated and the fingerlings raised. Nearly everyone who was raised in the region has a childhood memory of staring spellbound into the pools of squirming fish and feeding them with pellets from the adjacent vending machine.

On the main stem in Bethel, just above the confluence with the Third Branch, is the state-of-the-art fish hatchery that is the centerpiece of a national effort to re-introduce Atlantic salmon to the Connecticut River and its tributaries. To date, the effort has been less than successful. Two adult salmon were discovered in the summer of 2011. Unfortunately, one was discovered in the freezer of a fisherman who thought he had caught a large brown trout, and the other did not survive the flood.

Both hatcheries were heavily impacted by Irene as were many businesses. Facebook and YouTube emerged as characters in this play. Some would say for better, some for worse. Politicians clamored for the limelight. Unlikely heroes emerged. The road crews, the fire fighters, the volunteers, town managers, owners of excavators all have important moments on the stage.

For weeks at the barbershop, beauty parlor, post office, or general store, all people talked about was Irene. We're telling some of these stories once again on these pages, but we doubt it is for the last time. There may be no final chapter to this tale.

About the text and credits

A complete list of contributors including brief bios appears at the end of this book. The text consists almost exclusively of material previously published in *The Herald*. Following the title (or caption) are the date of publication and by-line. The articles are not presented in strict chronological order, but by where they fit thematically.

The overall organization is by watershed, by town, from West to East and North to South. (Reference map) Some towns (Stockbridge, Bethel, Royalton, South Royalton) are located both on the main stem White River and one of its tributaries and may be found in both places.

White River Watershed

State of Vermont

Courtesy of White River Partnership

Upper Branch White River
Granville
Hancock
Rochester

Tweed River
Pittsfield
Stockbridge
(intersects with White)

Third Branch
Roxbury
Braintree
Randolph
Bethel
(intersects with White)

Second Branch
Brookfield
East and South Randolph
Royalton
(intersects with White)

First Branch
Vershire
Chelsea
Tunbridge
South Royalton
(intersects with White)

Lower Branch White River
Stockbridge
Gaysville
Barnard
Bethel
Royalton
South Royalton
Sharon
Strafford
Hartford
White River Junction
(intersects with Connecticut River)

PART 1: The Calm Before the Storm

Weatherwise, *August 11*

Kevin Doering

The summer weather continued in full swing with another week in the 80s. We had fully reversed the soggy trend from late spring and early summer as mostly dry conditions prevailed and soil moisture levels plummeted. Now sections of garden needed water and lawns and fields began to show patches of brown. Light showers over the past weekend yielded only two-tenths of an inch of water and, for the first time in weeks, we genuinely needed a soaking rain.

Our lakes, ponds, rivers and streams have dropped from their record-high early summer levels and are providing wonderful recreation during these warm days of summer. Once again, the June through August period is averaging well above normal in temperature, while other areas of the southern U.S. are experiencing record heat and drought. I did see my first bats of the season this past week and am hoping that this is a good sign for their possible recovery here in Vermont. Some needed rainfall was falling mid-week, with generally cooler to reasonable temperatures.

AROUND THE STATE

5.8 Earthquake Felt in Central Vermont, *August 25*

Martha Slater

Earthquake! What earthquake?

When a 5.8 magnitude earthquake rumbled through Vermont at 1:55 p.m. on Tuesday, August 23, some residents were alarmed, and others said they never felt it. From all the reports we gathered, it appears that people sitting still were much more likely to feel it than those walking or driving at the time.

At *The Herald* office, the building began to shake and some ceiling lights swayed. Employees gathered in the front room and called down from upstairs as the tremors lasted for an estimated 15-30 seconds.

The strongest earthquake to hit the east coast in 67 years, it was felt in 20 states and parts of Canada. According to the U.S. Geological Survey website, quakes of this size happen about once a year in California, but only about once a century in this part of the world.

Although there were few reports of any damage in Vermont, the quake certainly got a lot of people's attention.

David Hurwitz of Randolph Avenue e-mailed *The Herald* about a half hour afterward, noting, "I was sitting here at my desk at home and I felt my chair rocking, then looked over and saw a floor lamp swaying, then heard stuff hanging on the back of my basement door swaying and clanking. That was a strong one! I felt the whole house swaying and moving."

Down Main Street at Ken's Barber Shop, Ken Jacobs said he had a customer in the chair, "when it started rocking and I checked to see if it was sitting flat on the floor." Many employees at Gifford Medical Center felt the quake, which made Tammy Hooker feel "dizzy and my stomach felt unsettled."

Folks from towns along Route 100 also reported their observations.

"There were three of us here and we heard squeaking, our chairs were moving, and the lights were swaying," said Pittsfield Town Clerk Patty Haskins, who also noted that the water in her water bottle was vibrating.

Up the road in Rochester, Connie Mendell was sitting at her desk at Occasions Catering, "and I thought my daughter's dog was under the desk making it shake back and forth! When I talked to my dad in Pennsylvania afterward, he said the windows in the building next door to him had all cracked."

> *Here's a glimpse of what life was like throughout the White River watershed.*

New Granville General Store Has Grand Opening Labor Day, *August 25*

Martha Slater

When the Granville General Store opens at 6 a.m. on Labor Day the town will have its first grocery store in more than a decade.

The former home of the Vermont Wood Specialties gift shop, the building had been sitting vacant after it closed seven years ago.

"Between the permitting process and getting the renovation work done, it's been like shooting a moving target, to find the actual date that we can open," said store owner Danial Sargeant, an energetic young man in his 20s.

He explained that the drive behind his new business venture was that, "I wanted a job in town and I didn't want to commute. My family has been here for seven generations and I wanted to stay here and create something for future generations. I think a general store is the base of a community—a place where everyone can go."

A member of the Granville Volunteer Fire Department, the Valley Rescue Squad, and the Moss Glen Grange, Sargeant is obviously involved in his community, and he wants his business to be, too.

White River (Upper)

Granville

Rochester

New Show at BigTown Gallery Showcases Adams and Ziek, *September 25*

"Geomancer," a show of paintings by Pat Adams and weaving by Bhakti Ziek, is on display at the BigTown Gallery on Main Street in Rochester through September 25.

In the mixed-media paintings of Pat Adams (oil paint, grit, shell, paper, foil) and the recent textiles of master weaver Bhakti Ziek (hand-painted silk threads, wool, cotton, textured yarns, digitally manipulated photography), one witnesses the similarity of abstract shaping and the layering of language, color, and texture.

Their large and small worlds are intricately detailed and concretely physical, defining metaphysical and emotional landscapes.

Tweed River

Pittsfield

Stockbridge

Pittsfield Volunteers Pack Up Library

Marion Abrams, Trustee Chair, Roger Clark Memorial Library

After quite a few years of discussion, some cordial and some heated, Pittsfield has finally decided it's time we meet ADA, clean up the mildew, and fix the roof of our old schoolhouse.

The old schoolhouse is now the home of our all-volunteer Roger Clark Memorial Library; soon it will hold fresh town offices on the first floor, and the library on the second.

We looked at rates for storage for the library books, and quickly decided that money should be spent on books and programs for our community, not storage space. Would you believe we've managed to pack up the whole library, and we're not paying one cent for storage?

That's right. Other than exactly the cost of a few cardboard boxes and $150 cash, your volunteers packed up and stored your entire library.

And we weren't alone. Did you know your volunteer firefighters don't just put out fires? They spent hours last week packing up the old school house. Pretty cool.

So, we care that much about providing our town with a great space, great books and great programs. We know you do too, and enjoy a great party, so please reserve your spot for our annual fundraising party at the Clear River Tavern.

Last Mile Ride
Raises $48,000, *August 25*

Gifford Medical Center's sixth annual Last Mile Ride attracted a record 219 motorcyclists, 23 cyclists and raised $48,000 for end-of-life care.

The charity motorcycle ride was the Randolph hospital's sixth annual. Since its start in 2006, rider numbers and money raised have climbed significantly. That first year, just 74 riders turned out and $7,000 was raised.

The steady climb in dollars raised for the cause is due to the support of sponsors, including many area businesses, and riders' fundraising efforts. Riders who raise the most win prizes.

This year, rider Larry Richburg of Randolph took the top prize of a $300 gift card to Wilkins Harley-Davidson in South Barre, after he collected more than $2,000 for the cause.

Said Richburg: "I can't believe the number of people who just call and say 'I have a check for you.' It kind of goes to show what kind of fundraiser and project this is. You don't find that very often."

Third Branch

RANDOLPH

Second Branch

Brookfield

Rally Crowd Supports Floating Bridge Repair
August 25

M. Dickey Drysdale

A crowd of at least 75 people turned out Sunday noon at Brookfield's Hippo Park to support local efforts to get the state of Vermont to repair the Floating Bridge.

The historic bridge—a tourist attraction as well as a state highway—has been closed to vehicular traffic for four years, as it was deemed to be unsafe. The flotation devices have apparently taken on water and the bridge is floating lower and lower.

Area residents are growing frustrated over the delay in preparing plans to repair it. In fact, there is a strong suspicion that the state just doesn't want to fix it, period.

Chelsea Selex Approve Committee To Reestablish Old Home Days, *August 25*

Heidi Allen Goodrich

Five citizens have joined together to begin planning a town-wide celebration next summer. No date has been set, but the group is looking at late August, before school begins.

Old Home Days celebrations in Chelsea's past have been elaborate three- and four-day affairs. The last celebration was held in 1974, according to the group. However, this committee envisions next year as a one- or two-day event that will be low cost to families and bring the community together.

First Branch

CHELSEA

Bell Ringing, Library Celebration
Celebrate 250th in Tunbridge, *August 25*

TUNBRIDGE

Scott Beavers

At precisely 6 p.m. on September 1, the bells in Tunbridge will be ringing.

As part of the town's ongoing 250th birthday celebration, the North Tunbridge Baptist Church, the village church, and the South Tunbridge Methodist Church will each ring their bells 250 times beginning at 6 p.m. Watches will be synchronized ahead of time and volunteers will ring the bells simultaneously. The time of day was chosen so that a good number of residents might be home from work and able to participate in and hear the ringing. The bell in the village church was cast in the 1840s and the North Tunbridge Church bell in 1870.

The bells are rung when church is held, but were also rung on the state and national bicentennial, at the end of World War II, and some people say they heard one ringing the night the Red Sox won the World Series in 2004.

After the bell ringing, everyone is invited to gather at the parsonage lawn, across the road from the village church, at 6:30 p.m. for a potluck supper as part of a celebration of the new Tunbridge Library's 10th birthday.

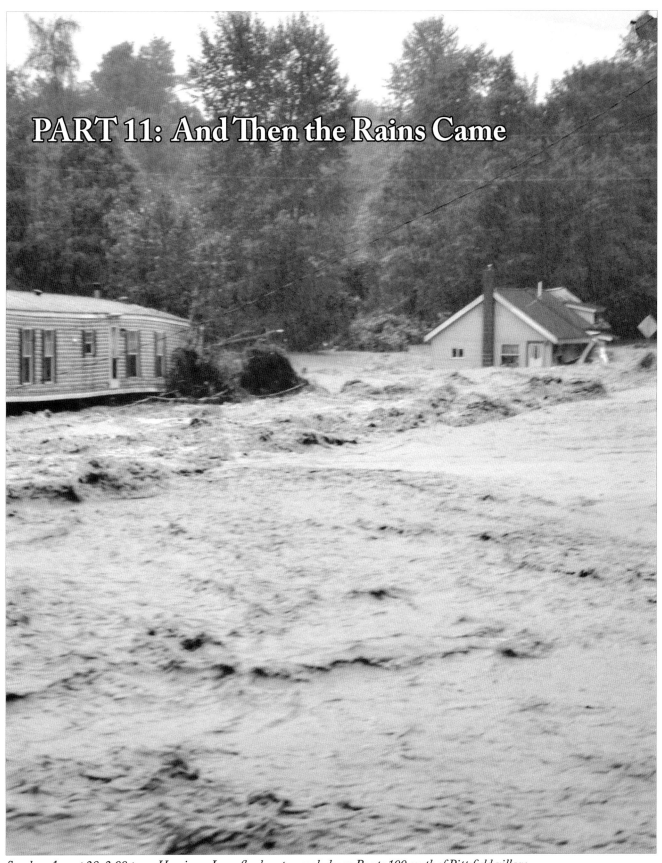

PART 11: And Then the Rains Came

Sunday, August 28, 2:00 p.m. Hurricane Irene flood waters rush down Route 100 south of Pittsfield village.

At 4:00 p.m. on August 28, floodwaters covered the bridge at the junction of Routes 100 and 73 on the outskirts of Rochester village. Within an hour later, the bridge collapsed.

Weatherwise, *September 1*

Kevin Doering

The following observations were taken in Randolph Center during the week of August 22-28, 2011.

	Low	High	Comments
Monday	58°	72°	mostly sunny
Tuesday	47°	71°	sunny
Wednesday	59°	80°	another great summer day
Thursday	59°	75°	occasional rain-.5 "
Friday	59°	80°	Irene nears
			North Carolina as category 2 storm
Saturday	57°	82°	Irene, category 1 along Virginia coast
Sunday	56°	69°	tropical storm hits Vermont, 7.56" rain

> "*Rain totals ran from 2.5 inches around noon to 7.56 inches just five hours later!*"

With all due respect to the sunny weather from the rest of last week, I will focus on the extraordinary, historic Tropical Storm Irene that Vermonters endured on Sunday. Many of us are still dealing with its enormous impacts—road and bridge washouts, flooding of homes and businesses, lack of power and, in many cases, lack of any modern measure of communication. Even at my hilltop location, midday Tuesday, a neighbor stopped to let us know that schools had been closed in Randolph until after Labor Day. She was passing the word along above the whine of generators in the Center, and this Vermont, neighborly approach was necessary, due to lack of power, phones, and computers.

Irene was a category one storm when it struck North Carolina, but amazingly, held its power despite being over coastal land areas all the way up to New York City. From there, it roared into New England as a tropical storm. Vermont faced some of its heaviest downpours. Rain totals ran from 2.5 inches around noon to 7.56 inches just five hours later! The already-saturated ground could not handle the copious rainfall, and rapid runoff into brooks and streams, compounded by elevation, induced speed, and the weight of this tremendous amount of water spelled doom for so many areas.

A few storm statistics from our area: Total rainfall, 7.56 inches; August rainfall, 15.19 inches; Lowest barometric pressure recorded Sunday evening, 28.81 inches; Peak wind, 23 mph sustained ENE, with 41 mph gust N Sunday night.

September 1 Editorial
What You Can't See

M. D. Drysdale

If you can see something, you can deal with it. It's what you can't see that can upset your world.

This has been a disorienting four days for Vermonters. Irene challenged assumptions that we didn't even know we had: Hurricanes don't come to Vermont. We can count on getting to the next town. We can count on making a telephone call. We can count on turning on the tap and getting water. If we don't know something, we can Google it.

Sitting at home Sunday, we didn't see a problem. Nice rainfall, not much wind. What we didn't see was the enraged Third Branch charging through the Prince Street commercial district, the Little League fields totally under water, the deep gash on Brook Street.

We didn't see the washouts on Thayer Brook or Riford Brook—and the washouts beyond them. We didn't see our friends who lived along the five miles of road that connect them. We didn't, couldn't, see the village of West Braintree,

the fractured Route 12A, the places the road plunged into a creek.

We didn't see one of our major highways, Route 107 out of Bethel, because it had disappeared. And we didn't see, or even hear from, Rochester and other Route 100 towns.

We didn't see the hill communities where residents were suddenly stranded, but we began to imagine they were everywhere. There was much more that we didn't see, and all of it was discomforting.

That's not fair. There was much that was happening this week that was encouraging, elevating even. People who were stranded decided to be stranded together. They had town meetings to decide what to do. Neighbors turned out to help their neighbors, strangers, too. People who met with disaster met also with kindness.

Still, it was a disorienting week, and the impression remains that what you don't see can be scary. Next week there will be more rebuilding, and we'll want to see it happen.

Top left: Irene turned Randolph's Recreation Field into something more suitable for canoes than bats and balls.

Top Right: Less than two miles south of Tozier's Restaurant, Route 107 between Bethel and Stockbridge was obliterated by flooding as far as the eye could see.

> *People who were stranded decided to be stranded together.*

Floodwaters from the Guernsey Brook created a cavern on Route 100's Pittsfield/Stockbridge town line, cutting off Pittsfield to the north.

National Coverage: Dateline Vermont, *September 1*

Vermont found itself in the national news. The Associated Press characterized the flooding as the "worst in the century" for Vermont.

CBS News called it "epic." In a front page story titled "Storm's Push North Leaves Punishing Inland Floods" the *New York Times* reported "250 roads" washed out and "several bridges." Those estimates proved to be grossly understated.

"We prepared for the worst and we got the worst in central and southern Vermont," Governor Peter Shumlin said on Monday. "We have extraordinary infrastructure damage."

At one point it appeared that the capital of Montpelier would be flooded as the local water company would be forced to release water to save the Marshal Reservoir, a local dam where waters were reaching record levels.

A historic covered bridge was swept away in Lower Bartonsville. The towns of Wilmington and Ludlow (among many others) were devastated. Flooding on the Winooski River inundated the village of Waterbury, forcing Vermont Emergency Management to move its brand new, state-of-the-art operations center to Burlington. Most other state offices were flooded as well. The state hospital was evacuated and its patients relocated to other facilities around the state. East-to-west access to Rutland was impossible. Emergency Management Spokesman Robert Stirewalt said an estimated 263 roads were closed across the state and at least nine shelters were set up. "This is the worst I've ever seen in Vermont," said Mike O'Neil, director of Vermont Emergency Management, quoted on CBS.

Irene: Clips From Around Vermont, *September 1*

Stephen Morris

Nearly every community around the state is coping with issues of infrastructure damage and community isolation. Here are some examples of how Irene's impact was felt across Vermont:

At least three of the state's iconic covered bridges were lost. Governor Shumlin promised they will be rebuilt.

Director Craig Fugate of FEMA surveyed the damage in the state and the Federal Government declared a state of emergency in Vermont.

Social media such as Facebook proved a double-edged sword, both in spreading mis-information and rumors, but also in correcting them. Residents of Montpelier panicked when it was reported that Green Mountain Power would be releasing water from the reservoir that would flood the downtown, later corrected by the official Montpelier town page on Facebook. (Of course, once the power went out, social media became irrelevant.)

Widespread road washouts and damage to bridges brought new meaning to the Vermont phrase "You can't get there from here." At least ten towns around the state, including Rochester, Pittsfield, Strafford, and parts of Stockbridge, were still completely isolated, unreachable by any road, 48 hours after the storm ended.

Emergency by-passes were needed on Route 4 in Mendon so that CVPS vehicles could reach downed power lines.

As the rain subsided shortly after 5:00 p.m. on August 28, the Rochester farm owned by Tom and Sandy Pierce was left surrounded by floodwater.

Brian Halligan evacuated his house on the south side of Pittsfield village just 20 minutes before it collapsed.

300-400 people were still stranded at a Killington Ski Lodge.

Scores of area businesses were damaged or closed by Irene, ranging from Bethel Mills (the state's oldest business) in Bethel to the popular Cottage Restaurant in Woodstock to the Alchemist Brewery in Waterbury to Dixie's Restaurant in Sharon. Simon Pierce in Quechee suffered significant damage, but will re-open.

Top photo: Fallen power lines on Route 14 near Welch's Hardware on August 29.

Rochester's electric substation was totally damaged by flood waters and floating debris.

Power Outages Plague Region, CVPS Responds
September 1

M. D. Drysdale

As of yesterday, the loss of electric power remained a central problem in Orange and Windsor Counties, as citizens struggled to return to normal. According to a state website, Orange and Windsor Counties led the state in the number of people whose lights were still off. Windsor had 5693 unserved customers and Orange County 2956. Randolph and Rochester had more electrical disconnects than any other town, with 2855 and 1291 respectively.

Crews and support staff have been working 18- and 20-hour shifts since before the storm began, and will continue to do so until the restoration work is done.

White River: Upper Branch

We were trapped here in the village. Even the cemetery opened up and caskets were going down the river.

Rochester Pulls Together Amid Tremendous Damages, *September 1*

Sandy Vondrasek

"We're in a world of hurt over here," came the word from Rochester Tuesday morning, via a cell phone report from Martha Slater as recorded by Sandy Vondrasek.

The call was one of a series of reports filed this week by Slater, *The Herald's* copy editor, who lives in Rochester.

She, like others in the village, and in surrounding towns and neighborhoods, was without power and utterly cut off from the rest of the world due to washed out bridges and roads.

Good neighbors, resourceful citizens, and an extraordinarily collaborative spirit made the best of a terrible situation.

ROCHESTER

Here are the
chronological
highlights from
Slater's dispatches.

Caskets and crypts from Woodlawn Cemetery were strewn
in Rochester's Mason Brook.

'It's Bad', *Tuesday, August 30, 11:10 a.m.*

Martha Slater

 With no cell phone service in the village, Slater had to get to a mountaintop with a borrowed phone to place the call. The situation was grim Sunday and Monday, as the White River invaded the village.

 "We were trapped here in the village. Even the cemetery (south of the village) opened up and caskets were going down the river.

 "Beth Frock's and John Graham's house on Robinson Avenue fell right into river—he was in it at the time. He had gone in to retrieve documents. The house started to go in river, and luckily, Shawn Keown was able to pull him to safety.

 "The electrical substation is on its side—totally damaged.

 "While they waited for assistance from outside, the townspeople pitched in, organizing efforts via daily meetings starting Monday, at the church. The church was packed with hundreds of people. Selectman Larry Straus shared information about what was known about surrounding areas. He reported the Route 73 bridge south of the village was out—lying

The situation was grim Sunday and Monday, as the White River invaded the village.

like a boat ramp in the river, by one account—and West Hill was cut off.

"He told us that sections of Route 100, north and south of Rochester village were wiped out, the bridge at Hancock was gone, and the Granville Gulf totally impassable. To the east, a big section of Camp Brook Road in Bethel was, in his words, 'a canyon.'

"The church is acting as a soup kitchen, serving lunch, and the guys at Huntington House opened up and are feeding everybody for free. They said they have all this food and a gas stove.

"Many folks are pitching in to help people living at Park House.

"Several folks, including Kathryn Schenkman, Suzie Smolen and Annie McKay, surveyed residents to determine 'severe medical needs' and are working in collaboration with Gifford Medical Center to get those needs met.

"The town road crew and volunteer citizens with equipment are working around the clock to reopen roads. It appears that a good number of folks, including town officials and workers, aren't getting any sleep at all.

"There are lots of generators in town, but we're running out of fuel and have no way to get more in. There are so many people heading up Bethel Mountain and other sites that the traffic is impeding the work of the local road crew.

"Selectmen are trying to reach AT&T, she said, to see if there were some way to get the tower in town working again.

"Food supplies are running low, and it has been decided to consolidate all free meal services at the school, which has a generator. Some people have been sleeping there.

"The town's water system still works, and it's not potable. You can flush once a day."

Starting the day after Irene passed through, daily community meeting were held at Rochester's United Church. On Tuesday, August 30, locals were able to meet with law enforcement and outside aid workers who brought food and medical supplies by helicopter.

Tri-County Public Safety Officer, Mark Belisle, holds an umbrella to shield Peter Parish as he pumps gasoline for Rochester residents waiting in line to power their generators, cars, and ATVs.

A Rochester Valley Story
September 1

Martha Slater

Stories of the Great Flood of 2011 from Hurricane Irene will be told for many years.

David "Duke" Hartshorn of Rochester told me about his frightening experience after being swept away during the height of the storm, on Sunday Aug. 28. Having driven his pickup truck to Stockbridge to check on an uncle there, he was heading back home, driving north on Route 100 a couple of miles south of town.

"The water was coming up fast!" he recalled. "My truck went off the road into a field from the force of the water and I hit a hole."

With water up to his waist in the truck, Hartshorn, who is 75, decided to swim for it to the closest help he could see, the home of Don and Joyce Jones on a knoll higher than the road level.

"I was in the water for a long time and it got darker and darker," he said. "I lost track of time."

Hartshorn finally made it to the Jones house, where he collapsed. Joyce Jones put warm towels around him and a thermometer registered his body temperature as 94 degrees. He stayed overnight there, and his worried son Mike, whom he lives with, was able to get through to pick him up the morning.

Medicines Over the Mountain, *September 1*

M. Dickey Drysdale

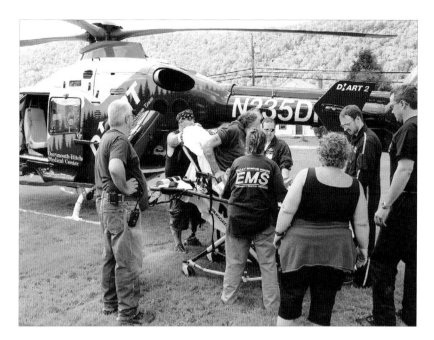

With the help of Gifford Medical Center and the White River Valley Ambulance, isolated Rochester received a crucial supply of medicines Tuesday afternoon.

A caller from the Rochester valley, which has no cell phone service and remains totally cut off from the rest of the area, managed to get through to the Medical Center Monday night at about 11 p.m., according to Gifford President Joseph Woodin. The caller said that organizers of the ad hoc village meeting in Rochester had identified nine residents there who were in urgent need of medicines.

The needs ranged from replacing dwindling supplies of regular medicines to dialysis treatments needed by four patients.

The hospital immediately started work to prepare a shipment of the needed medications. This involved, noted Linda Minsinger, working with Rite Aid to authorize and fill prescriptions on an emergency basis.

The list of patients in Rochester grew longer the next day, with about 25 included. Some of them were visitors in Rochester who had not gotten their prescriptions through Gifford, so the effort involved calling "all over the place," including other states, to get valid prescriptions.

The other challenge, of course was to get the medicines to Rochester. The answer was a four-wheeler vehicle that is part of the fleet at the White River Valley Ambulance. It was determined that if the medicines could be brought to the foot of the Camp Brook Road and carried or tossed over the ravine there, that the four-wheeler could make it to Rochester for the deliveries.

So about noon on Tuesday, Drs. Mark Jewett and Bill Minsinger drove to Camp Brook with the medicines and transferred them to the WRVA four-wheeler, which proceeded up the mountain.

Those receiving the shipment had to walk a ways to meet the four-wheeler at the Watershed Road area. Once in Rochester,

Linda Minsinger noted, the medications would be supervised by a medical team including four nurses "and a couple of visiting doctors."

The dialysis patients, however, were scheduled, as of Tuesday, to be airlifted out of the Route 100 valley.

Minsinger noted that a regular schedule has been set up so that there would be a phone conversation every two hours. That apparently took some doing, as the Rochester communicator had to get to a high point in order to get a cell phone signal.

The DHART helicopter airlifted those in need of medical care to Dartmouth Medical Center while a National Guard Black Hawk helicopter and crew provided transportation to Rutland Regional Medical Center.

Tweed River

PITTSFIELD

Texan Visits Pittsfield: So Does Irene, Part 1
It Was the Wrong/Right Time to Visit Pittsfield!
October 27

Candace Leslie

> *What we initially thought was thunder turned out to be rocks crashing together as they were swept up in the raging water.*

The rain began late Saturday afternoon, the fourth day of our stay in Pittsfield at what local folks refer to as "Sue's camp house." It had been an ordinary few days–trips to the grocery, blueberry picking, lunch in Rochester. The only real "work" had been to go through drawers and big plastic containers to sort out the keep-giveaway-toss stuff from Sue's and Mother's many happy summers in the old house. (We emptied six big containers, which would prove to be a rewarding effort in the days to come.)

Sue was not feeling well, plagued with a bad cold and dizzy spells, but she lay up on the bed and gamely made decisions

about things while I reorganized drawers and filled big plastic bags.

Thursday we began seriously listening to predictions concerning Hurricane Irene's possible arrival in the Northeast. By Friday the warnings had gotten somber enough that we moved up our planned trip to the Salvation Army in Rutland from the following Monday to that morning. After depositing some pretty good stuff at the SA, we stopped at Walmart to purchase their very last flashlight (a child's model with cartoon figures) and some Bonine for Sue's vertigo. We found one more mediocre little flashlight and a few batteries at the Dollar Store.

Carolyn (Buchele) Mallach arrived in Pittsfield from Albany late afternoon for a visit and stayed till Saturday afternoon, heading home to beat the brunt of the rains that would later plague New York state. I froze water in plastic containers so we'd have plenty of ice to keep perishables in the freezer compartment should the power go out. Karen Marion (our neighbor and guardian angel) had provided us with jugs of drinking water and I boiled well water as well. Sue filled a big container for flushing. We had plenty of food, and the house was up high enough to not be flooded by the beautiful clear brook (actually the West Fork of the Tweed River) that runs over the rocks below. We were ready!

My only concern was for the tall trees that surrounded the house. One had fallen two years earlier, and I knew they could be vulnerable in a high wind. I had no desire to be smashed.

Sunday morning we awoke to a

rising, rushing river, brown and angry, where the gentle stream had flowed the day before. What we initially thought was thunder turned out to be rocks crashing together as they were swept up in the raging water. Surprisingly, there was no wind and I was able to walk down the yard with an umbrella to take pictures at around 10 a.m. A little later, a neighbor who lived in a trailer across the side road came to see if we were OK and if we needed anything. A few hours later, the power went out. Then a fireman came by, looked things over, and assured us he thought we'd be fine. Still no wind, only more and more very heavy rain.

Then, around 4, a big ATV arrived with four firemen announcing they wanted to take us out to the village. They all agreed that flooding would not be a problem. But, "If anything happened and you needed to get out, you might not be able to. We might not be able to come get you. It's your decision." They gave us a few minutes to think about it and, if we decided to go with them, to get our things together.

First of all, we didn't want to put any rescuers at risk should we get in trouble. Secondly, I still worried about the trees. When the firemen returned, I asked their spokesman, "What would you advise if I were your mother?" His reply, "I'd say, GO!"

So we went. I had a flimsy raincoat that had belonged to Mother's long-late Aunt Marion. A young fireman gave Sue his big yellow rain parka and rode on the back of the ATV in the pouring rain. The firemen wrapped our two small suitcases in big plastic bags and stowed them in the back of the ATV. We climbed in front with the driver.

Top: Flood waters rise around the home of Heather Grevs and Jeremy "Jack" Livesy on the outskirts of Pittsfield village.

Left: Pittsfield Volunteer Firemen pull Heather to safety.

Bottom: Pittsfield Volunteer Firemen form a human chain to rescue Jack and his dog Kody.

Left: Jack with his mother Judi Livesy following the dramatic rescues.

Top: Not long after, floodwaters tear through the house and rush through the exposed kitchen.

Bottom: The house begins to disappear.

CONVENIENCE
STORE
- and -
U.S. POST
OFFICE
05762

Rick Stevens and his son Zack waiting for the National Guard to arrive in Pittsfield.

As we left the driveway, I could see water pouring in rivulets from across the road, making big loose ruts. We took the Upper Michigan Road which, too, was already washing out in places. People lined the road here and there, working with shovels to divert the growing streams of muddy water. The driver laughed and joked, assuring us he did have a windshield that he used in the winter, just didn't figure he'd need it in the summer. The rain drenched us, especially Sue, who had not had time to fasten the big yellow coat. Water ran down our legs and filled our shoes. It was a slow journey, but the rain, fortunately, was not cold. And still no wind.

The ATV left us at the Pitt Stop, the village gas station and convenience store. Here we shook off excess water and waited while Roger Stevens, the owner, gathered up some frozen pizzas, loaded us and them into his truck, and took us to the Swiss Farm Inn. Roger and his wife Joyce also own this ski lodge (locally referred to as "The

Swiss,") which is less than a mile down Route 100 from the center of Pittsfield village. Roger showed us to our room, via a flight of stairs and a long dark hall lit only by the fading afternoon light coming through a few open doors. Power had long been out in the whole village and surrounding area. We dried off and changed our clothes and shoes. Roger later brought containers of water for flushing the toilet (only as needed!). Then we worked our way downstairs to meet other "refugees" from Irene.

The first were a local family of a wife, two little boys, and the visiting mother-in-law from Cambridge, Mass. Their home, beside the river below the Lower Michigan Road, was in danger of being swept away. The father had stayed to watch over the house and was currently stranded in his truck. (Everything turned out fairly well for them–the husband got out, the house was slightly damaged, only the yard and garage were destroyed.)

Roger called us to supper, of necessity candle-lit. Pizza baked in

the big kitchen's gas oven, salad from bags, and soup from cans. No gourmet dinner was ever more welcome. Later we listened to weather news on someone's wind-up battery radio and I managed to make a couple of cell phone calls standing under a tree between showers.

The sky had lightened a bit, and it almost looked as if the storm were over. But as dark really settled in, the rain began again, and the wind began to rise. After visiting awhile with other refugees, we worked our way back to our room by flashlight. Roger gave me a cigarette lighter and as many tea-light candles as I wanted. I took six, by which we managed to get ready for bed.

Sue's cold was getting worse, but she was an amazingly good sport. I slept on and off, and finally, at first light, went down to the kitchen where Roger was frying bacon and eggs on his gas stove's griddle, slapping them between slices of white bread with a slice of cheese, and handing us the sandwiches on paper towels. A bottomless pot of boiled coffee cheered us all.

The storm was over. The sun was shining. It was a beautiful Vermont day.

During and After Irene, Pittsfield Village, August 28.

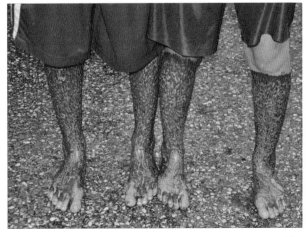

River rocks and sediment destroyed vehicles along River Road in Stockbridge. Beyond the car, the owner's home met the same fate.

STOCKBRIDGE

Havoc in the Hills

RAIN, RAIN, AND RESCUE: PART 1

A First-Hand Account of Surviving the Storm and What Comes Next, *September 29*

Tom Hill

I couldn't believe my eyes.

My jaw dropped in amazement.

I said, out loud, "Oh, my God."

In the days before Hurricane Irene had clawed its way up the East Coast, across the face of Vermont, and on toward Labrador, I had prudently stockpiled water, food, and batteries. But I had neglected one thing: gasoline. I had a small generator against the moment when the power would fail, but it wouldn't run on raindrops or sunbeams.

The hurricane had already brought confounded expectations: an almost eerie lack of wind, and a day of rain that was heavy and steady, but seemed no worse than anything delivered by your average slow-moving summer cold front.

When the power did go out, around 2 p.m. on Sunday, August 28, I had realized my oversight with respect to generator fuel. Driving down the steep, serpentine incline of Davis Hill Road in Stockbridge to Stony Brook Road below in the rain wouldn't be pleasant, but I'd done it many times before. Should the service stations out on Route 107 be out of gas, it would serve me right, but it seemed worth a try.

So I got into my car and began inching down the long driveway toward the short, narrow bridge that connected with the gravel road beyond.

What I found myself approaching as raindrops splashed against the windshield wasn't a bridge. It was a dark, yawning chasm, perhaps forty feet wide. The bridge was gone; the culvert was gone.

> *What I found myself approaching as raindrops splashed against the windshield wasn't a bridge. It was a dark, yawning chasm, perhaps forty feet wide. The bridge was gone; the culvert was gone.*

In their place, the babbling brook that trickled down the hill past my home had become the Raging Torrent From Hell. I disembarked and stood there in the rain, absorbing the spectacle.

A line of trees kept me from seeing the road itself. But all that water was going somewhere, and it had obviously jumped its banks before vanishing behind the trees.

With my brain already running behind the curve of obvious deduction, I backed my vehicle up and returned it to the carport. I went indoors and picked up the telephone—which, to my surprise, was still working. I called the two old friends in Kentucky from whom I was renting, and reported the situation.

To me, the situation was a washed-out bridge and a power failure. I didn't know the half of it.

Now, on the following day—having scrambled down into that ravine, leapt across the subsiding but muddy brook, and scrambled up the other side (almost breaking a leg in the process)—I stood on that tuft of gravel and tried to process the view.

Davis Hill Road was gone. As far as I could see, about a half a mile downhill to a bend in the roadway, two deep channels gouged the terrain: the bed where the river belonged, and a new one the river had carved when it chose Davis Hill Road as the path of least resistance.

I scrambled back across the ravine, returned to the house, and tried to call Kentucky. This was no longer possible. The phone was dead. Deep in a sprawling cell-phone dead zone, I was cut off from the world.

So, by the way, was my companion: a high-strung, high-maintenance, spoiled-rotten toy poodle named Buddy, who already knew something was terribly wrong. With the survival skills of, well, a toy poodle, this dearly beloved little parasite would need perpetual tending and comfort in the days to come. Abandoning him was, of course, unthinkable.

Helicopter

I had seen the first helicopter fly by on Monday morning — some distance away, its markings indistinguishable, no chance of flagging it down. By sundown, three more helicopters had passed across the sky—or the same helicopter three more times.

It was somewhat comforting to know someone was surveying the damage. But it was unsettling to realize that this survey required multiple helicopter flights, over a wide area.

On Tuesday morning, after assuring Buddy that I would soon return, I bushwhacked into the woods, GPS in hand, hoping to find someplace down the hill where I could emerge from the woods to see how much of the lower road had survived. After several hundred yards of branches, bog and bracken, I spotted a break in the thicket off to one side, scrambled down an embankment, and emerged into the sunlight about half a mile down from my driveway.

I looked up the road; I looked down the road. There was no road. As far as I could see, both ways, the scene might as well have been a canyon carved by a liquid-methane tsunami on a moon of Saturn, four billion years ago.

Not a speck of gravel or sand; not a speck of organic debris. Nothing but boulders and bedrock.

Not a speck of gravel or sand; not a speck of organic debris. Nothing but boulders and bedrock.

Everything smaller and lighter than a fire hydrant was gone.

Dog and I would not be hiking out. I returned to the woods and thrashed my way back home.

Just before noon, as Buddy and I stood in the yard trying to figure out a plan, I heard voices coming from the direction of the roadway. Other than helicopter engines, these were the first sounds of humanity I had heard in three days.

I trotted down to the dangling end of my driveway, and hollered.

Two voices, a man's and a woman's, hollered back. Through the branches of several fallen trees, I saw their forms moving toward me up the riverbed.

It was the local constable and a young woman in hiking gear, who had volunteered her experience as a backwoods hiker to the business of finding out who was still up in the hills, and what their needs were.

I'm still drawing up my list of saints and saviors, but these two folks are at the top of it.

Stockbridge Man Saved from Raging Waters
September 8

Susan Pelletier

Art Sulham almost lost his life during the hurricane. He was trapped in a house at the bottom of South Hill Road in Stockbridge after installing a generator to help a neighbor. This was Sunday morning the day of Hurricane Irene. Art found himself trapped in the house because of rising waters. He watched his truck float down the road and was rescued by Ken Carter Jr. with the help of many others.

Art asked that this letter not be changed but printed as he wrote it:

I wish to express my most heartfelt thanks to God and to the following people:

Mark Pelletier and Dave Brown for keeping in touch with my wife. Karen Furman and Jill Holtz for food and dry clothes. To Willie Lynam, Will Larkin, Jeremy Rayner, Travis Coombs, and Amanda Carter, for manning the ropes.

Most of all, I want to thank Kenny Carter Jr. for having the courage to wade into the nasty, muddy, filthy water to reach me. Also to any others that helped in any way.

> Thanks again and God bless.
> Art Sulham

Stockbridge Is Organized; Here's How To Find Help, *September 8*

Following extensive damage in Stockbridge during last Sunday's flooding, the town has had to reorganize and relocate many of its services.

The Stockbridge town clerk's office has moved across the road to the former Teeny Toziers building, with temporary, expanded hours. "We have many resources available to help you and answer any questions you may have," says town clerk Cathy Brown.

For now, daily meetings are held at three sites: The Meeting House on the common at 9 a.m., at Gaysville Post Office at 10:30 a.m., and the school at 6 p.m.

There is a food shelf at the Stockbridge School and another at the Meeting House, open to all Stockbridge residents.

"As long as all the roads are in such delicate condition, please come to the pantries to 'shop' and socialize," said organizers. "We have everything from soup to nuts, and help and assistance with just about everything."

Joanne Mills is the volunteer coordinator. Kim Robertson and Steve Farrington are tracking property loss in town and can assist you with the registration process if you wish. Ted Green Ford is providing a computer for this and there is also a computer available at the school.

Rob McFadden is tracking heavy equipment that is available. Please contact him if you have equipment available for town use.

Jen Harris is available to help with prescription needs.

There is a dumpster located next to the town garage on Blackmer Boulevard for household rubbish only.

Paul Buckley is monitoring the roads for the town.

Still badly battered from Irene's flood, Lillieville Brook Road served as one of the few routes between Bethel and Stockbridge. Neighbors joined together the day after the flood to start rebuilding the washed out River Road, making it possible for four-wheel-drive vehicles to ferry in supplies from Bethel.

Bethel's River Street is overcome by the raging White River.

The Wrath of Irene
Flooding Devastates Central Vermont, *September 1*

M. D. Drysdale

> *At about 11 a.m., however, the rain became a determined torrent, and it continued that way until mid-afternoon before dying out altogether by dinnertime.*

The rain began in the early hours of Sunday, about 5 a.m. or so, and for several hours it was steady but moderate, and entirely lacking in the winds that made Irene a Category 1 hurricane when she struck New York City the day before.

At about 11 a.m., however, the rain became a determined torrent, and it continued that way until mid-afternoon before dying out altogether by dinnertime.

The water began its work, but the flooding was not spread evenly over the watershed. Some areas—Braintree Hill, for instance, just received a soaking, while the Braintree ridge just to the west poured out furious bursts of water at every brook. Encountering a culvert or a bridge, the water tended to win out, finding a way around or over—many bridges were not actually destroyed but bypassed.

As the waters gathered into rivers, the Third Branch and the main stem of the White became the worst offenders.

Property damage was immense. The Herald has not yet been able to tally the damage, but there must have been at least 20-30 houses either destroyed or rendered uninhabitable. Businesses near river suffered the worst, such as the Abel Mt. Campground in Braintree and Bethel Mills; 800 cords of wood may have been lost in Bethel. Farmers were not immune; a farmer in Royalton lost most of his dairy herd, some plucked from the pasture and others trapped in the barn.

Third Branch

In West Braintree on Monday evening the only sound is of water running, spilling in cataracts over broken asphalt and down across rock littered front yards.

Large stretches of Route 12A in Braintree were destroyed.

A swath of railroad bed was wiped out by the flooded Third Branch of the White River on Route 12A below Thayer Brook Road. Some fifty yards of track and numerous cables were left hanging.

Abel Mountain Campground Leveled by Hurricane, *September 1*

M. D. Drysdale

One of the most disastrous results that Hurricane Irene visited on any private business in the White River Valley was the blow it struck to Paul and Karen Rea's Abel Mountain Campground on Route 12A.

Tucked down behind Mobile Acres next to the Third Branch of the White River, the campground has been one of the bright spots in Randolph-area tourism in the last few years. Every year, Rea comes up with an improvement or two, and a couple of years ago he added more than 30 new campsites for a total of 137.

Until Sunday, it had been a very good summer at Abel Mountain, with camper numbers up, and a new facility offering showers to guests.

On Sunday, however, Irene roared through, and left almost nothing in her wake, except for the 30 new campsites, which were built on higher ground.

Most of the sites were in a plain only 10 feet or so above the usual level of the Third Branch, and the most desirable of them were dotted right next to the river, where campers could listen to the soothing gurgle of the waters.

By afternoon Sunday, Rea could tell that trouble was coming, and all camper trailers were evacuated to the higher level (except one, which was destroyed). Rea also towed the new shower building to high ground.

The lower area of the campground was virtually leveled by the flood waters when they came. A pavilion building was destroyed, a snd an ugly gash flowed through the center of the campground. The camp office still exists in theory, but it was swept 100 yards east by the waters, and filled with four feet of soggy mud.

Rea said he has flood insurance, but only on the buildings. It is obvious that the whole campground has to be reconstructed. The new campsites are in better shape, but the river started cutting viciously into that higher meadow as well, making him wonder whether they are safe from future floods.

Rea received a steady stream of visitors offering their regrets all day Monday. In answer to the inevitable question, he said he is inclined to doubt he'll reopen the campground. But he's not sure.

"We've got a lot of thinking to do," he told *The Herald*.

Paul Rea walks to his office at Abel Mountain Campground. The building was pushed over 100 yards by floodwaters that filled the interior up to the eaves.

Until Sunday, it had been a very good summer at Abel Mountain, with camper numbers up, and a new facility offering showers to guests.

David Atkinson stands at the devastation above his property on Riford Brook Road in Braintree.

Neighbor by Neighbor, Riford Brook Rebuilds
September 1

Bob Eddy

Over centuries, Riford Brook in Braintree has slashed a ravine from the west down to the Third Branch of the White River. A road runs alongside the brook in this tight gash, and, for more than two centuries, folks have been living on the thin margins of negotiable land not occupied by the road and the brook.

On Sunday afternoon, as Irene's rain fell, those margins were tested. At David Atkinson's home, they all but disappeared. David knew his two-story dwelling was threatened by the middle of the afternoon. The roar of the water just behind his home was deafening. Still, his property had weathered the '98 flood. Like most of his neighbors, David felt this storm, too, would pass.

The end came swiftly. There was time to move the truck, grab his boots and wallet, but nothing more. The waters, rolling huge boulders and debris down from roadbed scoured above, dislodged clay and stone, and then the house. Left behind were David, one small bedroom connected to the main dwelling by a six-foot hallway and, further down along the bank, a shed with the tools for David's tree business. Gone were the kitchen, the Defiant stove, piano, bathroom, bedroom, and living room. Gone were thousands of photographs, books, letters, financial documents. In was a saga feared by thousands and lived through by many all over our state this week; David Atkinson lost almost everything he owned to the flood from Irene.

"I'm just so grateful that I still have my brother's bedroom, he enthuses as we enter the only part of his home still here. A few years back David took his ailing brother in, caring for him until his death. There was need for a first floor bedroom, which was added. "Thank God for this wonderful space," he smiles upon entering, "I just have to learn to live with less."

Less indeed. As my friend sifts through his few remaining possessions, delightedly pointing out prized flowers, trees and bushes clinging to the embankment, I am humbled by his simple heart and abundant faith.

> *The end came swiftly. There was time to move the truck, grab his boots and wallet, but nothing more.*

Top photo: David Atkinson uses a jerry-rigged ladder to cross the chasm at the end of Riford Brook Road. "I lost my land, my home, and almost everything I owned. I am learning to live with less."

Bottom photo: Riford Brook neighbor Stella Flint gives David a warm hug and blankets.

Randolph's Prince Street Doused by Irene

September 1

M. D. Drysdale

For dozens of Randolph residents, who congregated on the Main Street bridge early Sunday evening, in such numbers that at one point they were asked to move along, the scene below was unforgettable. The Third Branch writhed below like a demon, a filthy, angry, dark chocolate, moving with ferocity and breathtaking speed. It raced, not only in its channel, but around a leading edge of the flood wall onto Prince Street. On it ran, eagerly enveloping the buildings there, from Village Auto to the Once Again, Inc. store and First Choice Restoration, side by side, to the new restaurant, Chadwick's, the spacious new warehouse and offices of the Randolph Area Food Shelf and finally to the building housing Valley Bowl.

The last time the river overflowed so dramatically was during the 1927 Flood, when its ravaging of Prince Street marked the demise of an important Randolph manufacturer, the Sargent and Roundy foundry, makers of plows and other iron implements. Those standing on the bridge Sunday, watching the same river tear around and seemingly through the same buildings, knew that it was more than likely that the same fate had been visited on the present-day businesses.

By the light of Monday morning, however, the results of Hurricane Irene, though still grim, demonstrated some happy surprises.

Four businesses were indeed hit hard. Two of them, Once Again, Inc. and First Choice, took on water up to a height of four feet.

Two establishments—Village Auto and the Food Shelf—suffered an invasion of masses of mud and some broken doors, but little or no loss of essential equipment, and both were being coaxed back to life by a host of volunteer workers.

Most amazingly of all, two of the businesses suffered no water damage at all. The brand new Chadwick's Restaurant, and the popular Valley Bowl were ready to be back in business just after a thorough clean-up.

> *The Third Branch writhed below like a demon, a filthy, angry, dark chocolate, moving with ferocity and breathtaking speed.*

RANDOLPH

The rushing floodwaters of Camp Brook eroded the bank-side property of Gregory and Audrey Turk.

Bethel Takes A Hit

Camp Brook Road Repair Is Priority, *September 1*

Stephen Morris

Information was hard to come by on Monday morning in Bethel. Although the sky was blue and the sun shining, the community was badly disrupted by the heavy rains of Hurricane Irene.

Town Manager Dell Cloud has experienced a number of storms, but nothing quite like this. "The central and western sections of town have been badly damaged," he said, "but I can provide only a thumbnail sketch. We're still trying to learn what happened."

Cloud said that the River Street Bridge was closed, as was Route 12 north of town by the Camp Brook Road, leaving Interstate 89 as the only passage between Randolph and Bethel. The North Road was also closed. Findley Bridge was closed.

Cloud also said that the water supply system had been compromised and urged residents to not only boil water but to conserve. "This has introduced a number of potential contaminants to the water supply."

By Wednesday water had been restored on a limited basis. Cloud continued to advise conservation.

> *Cloud also said that the water supply system had been compromised and urged residents to not only boil water but to conserve.*

BETHEL

The remains of Bethel's Camp Brook Road

Camp Brook Road, reduced by Irene to a two-mile one-lane hazard, remained closed to daily traffic from 8:00 a.m. to 5:00 p.m. for approximately two weeks of reconstruction.

Camp Brook Road Priority

The town clerk reported that as of Tuesday afternoon, the state and town are working jointly on the Camp Brook Road with the goal of having it open by evening so that emergency vehicles can travel to Rochester.

Cloud said that re-opening this road was the town's top priority, and he hoped it would be open by the end of the day. (One resident referred to the road as "Camp Brook Canyon.")

An Emergency Relief Shelter has been set up at the Bethel School cafeteria. They are accepting all donations of food/bottled water, clothes, blankets/sheets, batteries, first aid supplies, diapers/baby items, toiletries, feminine products, towels, pet supplies, and gift cards for groceries and gas.

One resident referred to the road as "Camp Brook Canyon."

Gilead Brook Road

Gilead Brook Road was closed as of 3 p.m. Sunday. It is open to local residents only up to the 1.5-mile mark, but is impassable thereafter. Access for Macintosh Hill residents is possible via the Tatro Hill Road.

Many residents in Upper Gilead are stranded without electricity or phone service.

On the Wright farm, they are able to milk their herd with the assistance of a generator, but since the milk trucks cannot get through, they have to dump the milk.

Cases of bottled water have been left at Shirley Young's house on the corner of Gilead Brook and Macintosh Hill roads and are free for the taking.

Updates on the Gilead Brook community are being posted at BethelGileadvt.org.

> *On the Wright farm, they are able to milk their herd with the assistance of a generator, but since the milk trucks cannot get through, they have to dump the milk.*

History Is Personal and Comes at a Price

September 1

Shannon Trigos

> *I saw Leslie part sadly with her own mother's precious heirlooms. She pulled her clothes from trees.*

Shannon Trigos of Randolph Center spent Monday morning helping Mike and Leslie Piela of Bethel clean up what was left of their home. It had survived the 1927 flood, but was washed away by Hurricane Irene. This is her account:

1927 seemed like long ago, until Monday morning when I helped my friends sort through their few remaining belongings after Hurricane Irene had unleashed her fury.

Their house was the closest to the River Street Bridge in Bethel. The structure survived the 1927 Flood, but was moved to the other side of the road for safe keeping. Now it is probably in bits and pieces, somewhere in Connecticut, along with the Pielas' boat, clothes, furniture, and most of their keepsakes.

We waded through the muck and mire, salvaging what we could, ending up with three pick-up truckloads of belongings. Not much. We rinsed off inch-thick mud from picture frames to see what images they held. I watched as my friends relived memories of children during their school days. I saw Leslie part sadly with her own mother's precious heirlooms. She pulled her clothes from trees.

Here were people wading through memories and discarding many of them into the "junk pile." The neighbors, who had rushed into the house to gather belongings just before the house broke in half, now stood on the sidelines of what used to be a road, offering what help they could. There was a mixture of pictures flashing, people crying, people laughing, people yelling.

I dug through a jewelry box which was filled with silt, and found a Tigger pin. I washed it off, scraped out the silt with my fingernails, and pinned it to my friend's shirt. Trying to keep things as light as possible, I suggested we use the pink stethoscope hanging in the tree to see if the tipped-over car had a pulse. There was a box of Hungry Jack pancakes where their back yard used to be. Maybe we could whip those up for lunch? Now the back yard is a graveyard to a lifetime of memories.

When I finally went home and showered, I sat down to a warm cup of coffee and stared as I replayed the scene in my mind.

"We are making history," I thought. But there is so much more involved than just events and dates. There are hearts and souls and lives affected in every way. Helping hands and caring people throughout the community and surrounding towns coming together in loving support.

"And someday a group of friends may be sitting around sharing snacks and talking about the 2011 flood as if it were just another moment in time, but one we hold tightly in our memories because we were part of it."

The River Street home of Mike and Leslie Piela survived the Flood of 1927, but not Irene.

The River Street home of Paul and Dietra Feeney.

Cloud suggested using the town hall as a central location for volunteers. Levesque opened the doors there at 10:30 a.m. Thursday, and immediately the phone began to ring.

Huge Grassroots Volunteer Effort for Flood Victims in Bethel, *September 8*

Amy Danley-White

When Tropical Storm Irene hit Bethel, the town government and infrastructure started the monumental task of evacuating people, getting access to areas and people who became isolated by the storm, and addressing the water and sewer problems.

Other needs became apparent to townspeople soon after the flood. People didn't have access to hot food, clean clothes, places to stay, and manpower to help clean out houses and businesses of water, mud, and ruined personal belongings.

Several Bethel citizens realized that town services were overwhelmed and the only way to get help to people in crisis was through organizing volunteers.

Enter Sandy Levesque and a host of other volunteers who created the Bethel Disaster Clearing House.

Town Manager Dell Cloud appointed Levesque to spearhead the volunteer effort.

Levesque said, "I realized there was a need for volunteers to help out in town when, on Tuesday morning, I couldn't reach my Gilead neighbors who needed help.

"I work for myself and I have a flexible schedule so I called Dell Cloud at the town manager's office and asked if he needed volunteer help. He told me he would get back to me. I got a call back from him on Thursday morning, asking if I could coordinate volunteers, because he had limited manpower and communication access to do it at the town offices."

Cloud suggested using the town hall as a central location for volunteers. Levesque opened the doors there at 10:30 a.m. Thursday, and immediately the phone began to ring.

"I would answer the phone," she said, "and when I put the phone back down on the receiver, immediately

Bethel's River Street in the wake of Hurricane Irene

Volunteers help Paul and Dietra Feeney remove items from their home on River Street in Bethel on Monday, August 29, after heavy rain washes away much of their property and destroyed the house.

Volunteer Killian White, daughter of Kirk and Amy Danley-White of Bethel, spent several days following the flood shoveling mud from the basements of River Street homes. A graduate of Bethel's Whitcomb High School and a student at Middlebury College, Killian felt compelled to help out her hometown.

> **"I can't even estimate the scores of volunteers we received."**
> **Sandy Levesque**

the phone would ring again."

Levesque said she coordinated with Mary Ann Batcheller and Paula Beal, who run the Bethel Food Shelf, usually open four hours a week.

"By the end of Thursday, we agreed to find more volunteers to man the food shelf, and have it open from 9 a.m.-5 p.m. daily until the need subsided."

Many donations first went to the Bethel school, but clothing and cleaning supplies began to be redirected to the town hall on Thursday.

"Crystal Washburn took charge of sorting and organizing clothes," Levesque noted. "By the end of the day, there were tables lining the auditorium with all the clothes sorted into gender and size, and the stage held all the bedding.

"The conference room on the ground floor became the storeroom for cleaning supplies and hygiene products." Volunteers thought there would be a tremendous rush for supplies, but people were home dealing with their damage, she noted.

The Bethel Facebook page proved to be a valuable communications link.

"We also made a lot of phone calls and used word-of-mouth to help organize volunteers and donations," Levesque explained. "Communication was a real challenge. There is no cell phone reception in downtown Bethel. The town hall phone has only one line, and it can only be used for local calls."

Organizational and emergency information was posted on white boards and a bulletin board in the town hall lobby. Included was information on people who were providing showers and accommodations.

"Kirk White, who did a lot of the organizing of the clean-up crews, used the boards as a reference for what areas needed help."

The town offices kept the effort supplied with handouts of flood damage information and numbers to call for help from FEMA.

Levesque, who needs to get back to work, said that Amber and Shawn Taft will take over the coordination task.

"The effort will continue until the need has been met," she said. "I can't even estimate the scores of volunteers we received.

"We have had locals, people from all over the state, and even some from Massachusetts and Connecticut, who came to help out."

Tiny Bethel Lympus Faces the Flood of 2011

The wreckage of this bridge was bypassed and a new temporary one built.

September 8

Dorothy Manning

We had been hearing for quite a few days that Hurricane Irene would hit Vermont. Saturday night we filled the tub and as many containers as we had with clean drinking water. We spent the day moving nearly everything out of our shed that sits down by the brook. We also prepared for the Pittsfield Federated Church services to be held in Lympus on Sunday morning.

By 8 a.m. Sunday morning it was raining lightly and we began to think that no one would be coming to the church services. However, we were pleasantly surprised by the fact that 26 people did indeed make it to church.

By the time services were over, rain was falling steadily and the brook was beginning to swell. When I checked the rain gauge around 10 a.m. it registered 4-1/2 inches. I emptied it, because it only holds 6 inches, and we thought this storm would bring us more than that. By noon the brook had risen above its banks, and our back yard looked like a river.

We lost our power shortly after that, but still had phone communication. We learned from our daughter in town that the trailer park by the school had been evacuated and that she had heard that they were thinking about evacuating River Street. I worried about our neighbors in Lilliesville.

Campbell Brook Road had several washouts and the bridge to Lilliesville was impassable because the road around either side of it had washed out. There were also trees on power lines in several places.

People from around the community traveled on foot or by ATV to check in with each other.

Monday afternoon, I was walking up Campbell Brook Road with Bernice and Norman Martin when a large maple tree startled all of us by nearly landing on us. Fortunately, we were all able to get out of the way in time, but it was a truly frightening experience.

While there was a great sense of community and people visited and worked to keep each others' spirits up, it is a horrible feeling to be isolated from the world. We did not know how things had fared in town and were unable to communicate by phone, receive mail, or hear from the mailman how things were elsewhere.

Even though we were not able to get into town, we still had our lives and our home, we could rest assured that life would return to some semblance of what we had known before Hurricane Irene. Neighbors were now regularly using ATVs to get out and had brought us the newspaper, cat food and milk. On Thursday, neighbors even brought us a copy of *The Herald*.

> *While there was a great sense of community and people visited and worked to keep each others' spirits up, it is a horrible feeling to be isolated from the world.*

Disappearing cornfields, south of Bethel on Route 107.

Agricultural fields along the White River in Bethel buried under thick layers of silt.

Justin Cassidy rests on a flood-soaked car during his family's trek from his Camp Brook home in search of "civilization."

> **Small kindnesses may ultimately be the legacy of Hurricane Irene.**

"I Think I Hear Your Family," *September 1*

Stephen Morris

Nancy Cassidy was at work at *The Herald* at 12:30 on Monday when she received a cell phone call from her granddaughter, Amanda. The connection was sketchy, but the message was clear. "We're walking out. We'll meet you at Camp Brook Corner."

Amanda lives with her mom and dad (Shawn and Stephanie Cassidy), her brother Justin, dog and cat (Ozzy and Nina respectively) on Brink Hill Road, which runs off of Camp Brook Road on the Bethel side of Rochester Mountain. They live in an isolated area but, like so many residents of central Vermont, they are well prepared for an independent lifestyle. When the power failed, they turned on the generator. When the pond above them overflowed, washing out the base of their driveway with an 8-foot deep hole, they settled in for the duration. But when the generator blew up, they decided it was time to head for civilization.

While Shawn navigated his family down to the main road, his mother drove down to meet them. Initially, she could get only as far as Onion Flats on Route 12, heading south, but then discovered if she was willing to drive through six or so inches of mud, she could make it to the junction of Camp Brook Road. There a town employee with a neon vest was keeping vehicles from going further. She told him

her plight, and he tried to be as helpful as possible.

There wasn't much to do, however, but wait. Knowing that the family had a dog and cat, every time he heard a bark he'd say "I think I hear your family coming." Unfortunately, a yappy dog at a nearby residence insured many false alarms.

Shawn found the roads so washed out that even a four-wheeler could not negotiate a path all the way down, a trip that included a water crossing. Luckily, his knowledge of the snowmobile trails got the family down to the pavement.

Mom wanted to let the family know where she was located and met a young man about to embark by foot to Rochester to check on his family's welfare. He helped out by sending Amanda a text message of his mother's whereabouts. In gratitude she gave him the apple and granola bar she had brought for her own lunch. Small kindnesses may ultimately be the legacy of Hurricane Irene.

By 3 p.m., the family was united and the kids were safely ensconced, albeit still without electric power, in grandma's Randolph Village home. Shawn and Stephanie drove back to Camp Brook and walked home to bring out the cat and dog, finally arriving back in Randolph, after dark, just before the lights came back on.

Brookfield Crew Struggles To Save Homes Below Pond, *September 1*

Marjorie Drysdale

Brookfield's Pond Village was the site of frenzied activity Sunday night as members of the road crew and volunteers from the community struggled to save the homes of their friends and neighbors.

Richard Fink, who owns Ariel's restaurant on Brookfield Pond (also known as Sunset Lake), gave this account.

"We had the same amount of rain as everyone else did Sunday. Beth Urie recorded 10.5 inches at the top of Ralph Road. Ted Elzey had recorded 6.5 in the village.

"The dam couldn't hold such an enormous amount of water, so the water sought other avenues of egress. It went over the top and around both sides." This included the park where Jim Sardonis' hippopotamus statue stands, as well as on the other side of the road, where the Fork Shop stands.

"I was there with the crew as everyone tried to save the southeastern part of the village," Fink relates. "The water was beginning to pour down Route 65. It was frantic—lots of equipment right where it was all happening. Everyone was furiously digging trenches, worried that the dam might blow, head for the church and destroy every house in its path."

Leading the crew was Brookfield road supervisor Ray Peck. "At one point, Ray was on a backhoe in the middle of the torrent and the water was pushing at the tires on both sides," Fink recalls.

Wisely, Peck had anchored his rig with metal supports, preventing the water from pushing him downstream.

Jane Doerfer, owner of the property formerly known as the Fork Shop Restaurant, is extremely grateful for the crew's work, and attributes their efforts to saving her home. She ended up with just a couple of inches of mud in the storage room.

"It was a valiant effort," Fink said.

CVPS: Darkening Brookfield Was 'Switching Error,' *September 1*

M. D. Drysdale

CVPS officials in Rutland yesterday, responding to rumors and criticisms circulating in Randolph and Brookfield, said that Monday's shut-off of power to Brookfield and Randolph Center was a mistake.

The power to Brookfield was shut off at the same time late Monday that power to Randolph village and Gifford Medical Center was restored. The story quickly circulated that the Brookfield Ridge Road power had been diverted to the village, and tempers flared. The CV map confused Brookfield with West Brookfield.

Everyone was furiously digging trenches, worried that the dam might blow, head for the church and destroy every house in its path.

A member of the Royalton Fire Department surveys area damage early Monday morning, August 29.

> *If you see a road closed sign, but you don't see the damage, stay off the road.*

ROYALTON

Roads Closed as of Tuesday in Royalton and Vicinity, *September 1*

As of Tuesday at 2 p.m., the following roads in the Royalton/South Royalton area (either all or part of the road) were closed due to damage caused by the recent storm. If you see a road closed sign, but you don't see the damage, stay off the road. Road damage may have occurred further down the road or the damage may have occurred underneath the road surface, making the road unstable.

Route 14
Johnson Hill Road
North Road
Russell Road (sections)
Fox Stand Road
Fox Stand Bridge
Happy Hollow Road
Gilman Road
White Brook Road
Bridge Street
Royalton Bridge

Sharon/Strafford area:
Broad Brook Road (lower)
Route 132
Strafford Road
Tiger Town Road
Beaver Meadow Road
Mitchell Brook Road
Valley Road
Quimby Mountain Road
Belknap Road
Faye Brook Road
Steel Road

The Fox Stand Bridge off Route 14 in Royalton

45 Are Evacuated

First Branch Overflows, Chelsea Lucky

September 1

Heidi Allen Goodrich

Rumbles of generators and heavy equipment filled the valley of the First Branch of the White River, after Irene brought enough rain to overflow the riverbanks throughout the village on Sunday.

Despite the messy cleanup, most citizens were considering themselves lucky on Monday morning.

Chelsea's emergency response team evacuated around 45 people from the village, including residents of the Riverbend residential care home and the Brookhaven Treatment and Learning Center.

They found shelter at the United Church of Chelsea, where they enjoyed a dinner and spent the night on cots from the Red Cross while they waited out the storm, and the flooding.

The Chelsea Fire Department was on the scene Sunday to close down Route 110, just south of the creamery bridge where the river was running over the road.

That was the only road closure in Chelsea and was temporary, Fire Chief John Upham said, although on a few roads "it was close for awhile." There was also little or no structural damage in town, he said.

A few homes were completely surrounded by the river, and most homes adjacent to the river suffered flooded basements. The Fire Department spent Sunday afternoon and Monday morning pumping dozens of basements.

Many of these homes have been prone to flooding in the last few years. In 2009, a flash flood brought the First Branch above its banks throughout the village, and every spring, residents wait and watch the Jail Branch Brook with worry. Several times in recent years, ice jams in the brook have caused significant damage within the downtown area.

The flooding and power outages also spoiled plans for a First Day Parade on Monday. Chelsea Public School canceled its first and second day of school and does not know when the first day will be, because it is unknown when the power will return.

In Chelsea, damage was minimal and spirits were high. In the words of Selectboard member Jack Johnson, "We're d___ lucky!"

One reason, said Fire Chief Upham, was that this time, "Jail Brook behaved!"

> *"Jail Brook behaved!" said Fire Chief Upham.*

First Branch

CHELSEA

Irene Takes It Easy On Tunbridge, *September 1*

Scott Beavers

Relative to some other towns in Vermont, the damage in Tunbridge caused by Irene was not exceedingly bad.

A few roads washed out and power went out for many homes, but nobody was hurt, all the bridges are undamaged, and there were no reports of homes being heavily damaged.

Early on in the storm, there were problems with the Foundry and Larkin Roads, but they were resolved. The only longer term washouts are on the Strafford Road and Belknap Brook Road. Early Monday morning, work was already being done on the Strafford Road. Fire Department Chief John Durkee called a meeting Saturday evening with the road crew and all town officials to discuss the town's in-depth emergency plan.

A notice of potential storm problems, emergency services, and the evacuation shelter that was being set up at the school, was printed and distributed by Durkee throughout the town. The evacuation shelter at the school had cots, water and food provided by the Red Cross and although only one person took advantage of the shelter, Wendy McCullough, Kevin Moran and other volunteers manned it throughout the night.

The fire department's emergency plan was put into action Sunday morning and according to people involved, was extremely thorough, well thought out, and implemented perfectly. About 15 fire department volunteers, along with the road crew, spent the day and night dealing with issues as they arose.

Good Call

One of the first actions Chief Durkee ordered was moving the road crew equipment from its location on the Dump Road to higher ground and, sure enough, the first road to become impassible was that road.

Fortunately, the only major issues were road flooding, which first closed side road access to Route 110 and ultimately closed the state highway from the Wellspring School south to Russell Road. At one point they measured about four feet of water covering one part of Route 110. Once the rain stopped, the water receded from the fairgrounds, roads and other places about as quickly as it rose.

Homes along Route 110 in Chelsea are surrounded by floodwaters.

> *The fire department's emergency plan was put into action Sunday morning and according to people involved, was extremely thorough, well thought out, and implemented perfectly.*

TUNBRIDGE

A small work crew performs repairs on Route 12 in Barnard, which closed after the August 28 flood.

> *Five neighbors, she said, were sharing a generator, "everybody is taking around two hours."*

White River

Lower Branch

BARNARD

Barnard Roads, Bridges Knocked Out
September 1

Sandy Vondrasek

"We had the Hudson River going through where Locust Creek usually is," reported Jeanne Ward, of the scene Sunday on Route 12 in Barnard.

"We were isolated until midday yesterday (Monday)," she added.

Two Route 12 bridges were knocked out by high water, one about three miles north of Barnard General Store, and the second near the Route 107 junction.

The dam at Silver Lake, however, held, she said.

Ward said she understood that Route 107 "from Tozier's on toward Rutland" was badly damaged, as well as the Stony Brook area of Stockbridge.

By Tuesday afternoon, the Barnard road crew, with the help of residents, had patched badly damaged dirt roads, including Fort Defiance Road.

Also, a circuitous, back-roads route via Rousseau Road had been repaired enough to allow limited travel in and out of the area, Ward said.

Water damage was extensive in the valley, and it hit the Wards too, with the flooded brook carrying hay and firewood downstream.

Ward said she and neighbors were buoyed by acts of kindness, including offers of help from residents in other towns.

The power was still out Tuesday when Ward spoke with *The Herald*. Five neighbors, she said, were sharing a generator, "everybody is taking around two hours."

South Royalton Loses Roads and Homes, But Contact Restored, *September 1*

U. S. Representative Peter Welch stopped in South Royalton to see the flood devastation.

Pamela Levasseur

"Unbelievable" could have accurately described the gentle warm breeze, sunshine and picture perfect blue sky that followed the tropical storm that had just passed no more than seven hours earlier, overflowing the White River and nearby brooks and creeks with brute force that uprooted trees, swept a house from its foundation, crumbled concrete, and broke metal lamp posts as if they were toothpicks.

U.S. Rep. Peter Welch, stopping in South Royalton, was amazed.

"You guys have been hit really hard, you really have," the Congressman said. "I have very fond memories of this area, and not in my wildest imagination did I foresee this happening."

"It happened so quickly," said Nancy Murphy of South Royalton as she described the minutes just before she and her husband Bill knew they had to evacuate their home on South Windsor Street. Residents in the area were keeping a close eye on the river; they were taking precautions and moving their belongings that were stored in the basement up onto makeshift shelves just until the storm passed.

Some were used to getting their basements flooded. "It's something you have to expect every now and then when you live near a river," said one of the residents who asked not to be identified. This time was different, though.

The rain slowed down in the early evening, leaving some to believe it would give the river a chance to recede before the next wave of the storm.

"I thought the worst had passed," said one of the residents further down on South Windsor Street.

Once the river overflowed its banks,

> *The river was flowing into the basement faster than they could retrieve their family photo albums.*

SOUTH ROYALTON

the rest happened so fast. Henderson's Hide Away campground had worked steadily to move campers further away from the river in preparation for the storm. But a few of the recreation vehicles didn't survive the force of the river that swept them away. For the Murphys, that was only the beginning. One camper actually twisted around the corner of their house before being pulled about 50 feet further down their property, then crashing into another camper, and ending up smashed, mangled together and sunk into the more than five-foot-deep gorge that the river dug out of their back lawn.

The river was then flowing into the basement faster than they could retrieve their family photo albums. The mark on the wall showed how high the water reached above the basement steps and flowed throughout the remainder of their home.

The bottom row of kitchen cabinets had been filled with river silt left behind when the water receded. Every room

was left with inches of muddy silt that needed to be shoveled out. Furniture was being moved out of the house, much of it destroyed, carpets were being ripped up. The garage looked as though it had sunk into the deep mud. Family, friends, and volunteers were helping to move their belongings out of the garage.

As Nancy led me into the entryway of the dining area of their home, I just stood with a gasp that I tried to hide. The only words that came to me were "I'm so sorry."

Despite the shoveling and mopping, there was still a wet glaze of silt over the floor. Her voice was shaky as she pointed out the damage, as well as all the work already done with help from volunteers who just started to show up to help. "We are so grateful for everyone that is here to help."

"The help has been just amazing," said Nancy repeatedly. "Just amazing. I don't know what we would do without this help."

A substantial section of Route 132, about 1-1/2 miles below South Strafford village, was washed out.

Village Evacuated

Strafford Suffers Many Road Closings

September 1

John Frietag

Strafford was hammered by the hurricane, with many of the town's roads taking a big hit. On Monday, nine road closings were posted on the town's website.

Many of the roads included the main arteries out of town to Tunbridge, Sharon, and points east. Route 132 was closed in both directions.

The village of South Strafford was temporarily evacuated when propane tanks behind the store became unmoored.

Local contractors have been enlisted in the effort to open the roads.

There will be much work needed before all the roads will be opened and a great deal more needed before repaired to the condition they were in before the start of the storm.

Particularly hard hit were Alger Brook Road, Van Dyke Road, and Taylor Valley Road.

The Vermont Alpaca Farm lost its private bridge and two young alpacas.

Other private bridges destroyed by the storm include those of Rod and Cindy Maclay, which provides the access to Strafford Saddlery and to the site of the old Huntington Fence Company now owned by Eric Thorp.

The Vermont Alpaca Farm lost its private bridge and two young alpacas.

Chanda Aldrich surveys the damage done to Sandy's Restaurant on Route 14 in Sharon. A small army of volunteers helped clean the muddy mess.

Sign put up by restaurant staff on Sandy's mud-encircled storage shed.

> The fire department itself is inundated with several feet of water.

SHARON

In Sharon
Dixie's Restaurant Lost, Routes 14 & 132 Damaged, *September 1*

Stephen Morris

Selectman John Harrington reports that both Routes 14 and 132 suffered severe damage from erosion and have been closed to all but local traffic. Both roads have extensive loss of blacktop and are covered with mud.

Several area businesses were wiped out, including Dixie's Restaurant, a popular area gathering place.

A campground across from the fire department had to be evacuated, and there were sightings of camping vehicles being carried down the river.

The fire department itself is inundated with several feet of water and the vehicles are parked outside for the time being.

A doublewide trailer was also lifted from its foundation and moved down river.

The highest current priority is to re-open Route 132 to Strafford, which is currently isolated. The most pressing challenge at the moment, Harrington said, is traffic control, which is being handled by a combination of the fire department, road crew, and volunteers.

"If there's a silver lining," said Harrington, "It's that this disaster has brought out the best in people, and they are working well together."

A road restoration project that was recently completed at a cost of $275,000, reported Harrington, was lost completely.

PART III: A World of Hurt

Alex Riesterer carries his son, Arden, down the new streambed that used to be where Camp Brook road sat.

Weatherwise, September 8

Kevin Doering

The following observations were taken in Randolph Center during the week of August 29-September 4, 2011.

	Low	High	Comments
Monday	55°	71°	increasing sunshine, less winds
Tuesday	47°	75°	sunny
Wednesday	55°	76°	partly sunny
Thursday	55°	74°	mostly cloudy, light showers p.m.
Friday	55°	76°	partly sunny, more humid
Saturday	60°	85°	warm and muggy
Sunday	60°	87°	some sun to clouds and rain (.25")

Many Vermonters in our area continued to struggle to return to normalcy in the wake of Tropical Storm Irene. One couldn't travel far from the interstate in central and southern Vermont without noticing severe damage incurred from the torrential rain and consequent flash flooding, which saw streams and rivers rise 20 feet or more within hours of the onset of the tropical rains a week ago last Sunday.

What happened meteorologically? Why did this tropical storm provoke so much damage compared to storms of similar magnitude since the Great Flood of 1927? There are several factors that created this situation, and last week I noted that Irene retained much of its original strength despite a significant period of time over land. This was true because of its immense size. The storm, almost 500 miles across, crossed land on three occasions before striking New England. In North Carolina, however, and again farther north, a major portion remained over water, where its large circulation continued to draw in moisture. The path of the storm took it straight into Vermont, where the saturated tropical air from its western side met the Catskills, Adirondacks, and the Green Mountains. The tropical moisture and stronger rain bands already located in this area of the storm were forced upwards into colder air, forcing condensation and increasing the intensity of the rain. Essentially, the mountains wrung out additional precipitation from an already well developed low, resulting in 6-8 hours of very intense rainfall, producing quantities seen only every 50-100 years over much of eastern New York and southern and central Vermont. The reader may also recall that much of our area had received up to five inches of rain within the prior 10-day period, which meant that streams were no longer below normal levels as they had fallen to in early August.

Clean-up continues this week. Fortunately, forecasted rainfall this past weekend didn't quite reach the higher end levels that had been predicted. We are, however, facing still more rain from a warm front this week, which could also draw in some moisture from slow-moving tropical storm Lee. This rainfall was not expected to reach an intensity necessary for additional flooding, and as of this writing, Hurricane Katia looked to be moving well to our east, posing no threat to our area. Meanwhile, the school buses were out once again, signaling a new season on the horizon, one hopefully filled with relatively pleasant meteorological conditions.

*Carl Oertel picks up a piece
of blacktop that Irene freed
from the bridge over the
West Branch of the Tweed
River in Pittsfield.*

Labor Day Takes On a New Meaning, Editorial

September 8

Lisa Manning Floyd, Bethel

> *But this past week has shown me new respect for the blue collar workers of the community.*

This Monday marked Labor Day. It's a day I didn't fully understand when I was a kid and that I am not sure I fully appreciated until this year. I grew up in a family where work was valued; my father was treated for cancer for nearly a decade without taking a sick day.

My mother worked her whole adult life too, until retirement. And now, they still stay pretty busy. But this past week has shown me new respect for the blue collar workers of this community.

On Sunday afternoon, while Hurricane Irene was raging, Bethel volunteer firefighters were directing traffic and closing roads to keep people safe. Their family members were also hard at work getting people settled into an emergency shelter set up at the school and communicating needs to community members who were able to offer support.

But, unfortunately, Sunday was not the last day that people were in need. When the sun rose Monday morning it was clear that the emergency would continue for days for some, right through the winter months, perhaps, for others. Homes were devastated in pockets all over town. People up Camp Brook and on the end of Gilead and in Rochester and Stockbridge could no longer be easily reached by car.

But, the brave men and women of the BVFD and White River Valley Ambulance made their way to people in need. Trails were cut, and this crew was seemingly unstoppable. They brought the first supplies into Rochester and Stockbridge on convoys of ATVs.

Also, people with heavy equipment worked tirelessly to repair damage in their own small communities. Fixing damaged roads and putting streams back in their beds seemed to be the job of everyone who had the knowhow and equipment to do it. It

seemed like everyone was mobilized and sharing the workload, from offering counseling to cooking for the displaced and volunteers to helping muck out destroyed homes. Vermont labor was and is getting the job done.

At this point the town food shelf is full to overflowing. Clothing donations have poured in and the shelter has been moved to Randolph Center. Community suppers are planned for every night this week.

And, some small businesses that were affected have already re-opened. The hardworking people of Bethel have pulled together and I hope will pull through this emergency. When all is said and done there will be some time for reflection and plans for how to handle future disasters will need to be revised and strengthened. Still, I can't help but feel proud of the people who have acted and worked together to help move us forward from this crisis.

The other day I saw a picture on Facebook and it brought tears to my eyes; it's a picture of Tim Aldrighetti

rescuing Paul Chatfield from a car that was overcome by water.

I remember Tim best with a Whitcomb jersey on playing soccer years ago, now he has grown into a young man, who didn't wait for someone to tell him there was an emergency, or who worried about whether what he was doing was the right thing; instead he jumped in and got the job done.

There are several young men and women who grew up in this community who took action last week. On a normal week you can see them working in local pizza shops, at Bethel Mills, and for the state road crew. They are nurses at Gifford or workers for CVPS, receptionists, teachers and lawyers, and still they pitched in and worked side by side getting the job done.

The work isn't over for sure, but this past week and a half has proven that together we can get amazing things done.

(*We couldn't figure out a way to say it any better, or half as well, so thanks to Lisa for sending us this as a letter. Editor.*)

> *The other day I saw a picture on Facebook and it brought tears to my eyes.*

Around the State

Amy Zajdel and Justin Laramie were away for the weekend when Irene's floodwaters engulfed their house on Route 100 in Pittsfield. A family of rabbits on the back porch was lost, but Pancetta the pot bellied pig survived.

> *You are not registered until you get that nine-digit number.*

FEMA Message: When in Doubt, Register

October 6

Sandy Vondrasek

Around 6,000 Vermonters have registered with FEMA for disaster aid, in the wake of Tropical Storm Irene. Close to $17 million in FEMA grants for individual assistance have already been approved.

With 650 federal and state employees deployed throughout the state, the disaster response "is going very well," commented FEMA officer Victor Inge last week. A growing number of flood victims, he said, have sought out help at the mobile Disaster Recovery Centers touring the state.

"Lots of Vermonters have the feeling that they can take care of themselves; that their neighbors are worse off than they," commented Angela Drexel who is overseeing the FEMA response in Orange, Addison, Washington, and Rutland Counties. Drexel urged everyone "impacted" by the storm—including renters—to register by the October 31 deadline. Problems, including mold, might not develop or be detected until months from now—and then it will be too late to ask for help, they point out.

"You are not registered until you get that nine-digit number," Drexel emphasized.

Toll in Houses High for Central Vermont

A home hangs precariously over an eroded cliff in the Route 100 valley.

Nearly 100 Homes in White River Valley Are Unusable
September 22

M. D. Drysdale

The flooding that followed Tropical Storm Irene destroyed or rendered uninhabitable about 100 homes in the White River Valley, so far as *The Herald* could determine this week. Finding homes for the displaced residents, probably numbering 200-250, remains one of the toughest tasks of the recovery.

The dimension of the housing task is far less obvious than the very public task of rebuilding Randolph's Main Street 20 years ago after the series of downtown fires, noted Marty Strange last week. Then, the damage was to businesses, which were constantly visible to all. This time, much of the damage is to private homes, many of them tucked away

Mobile Home, Route 100, Pittsfield

> *In addition to those whose homes were wrecked by the flood, there are others who still cannot reach their homes by car or truck and may not be able to do so for months.*

next to brooks, he reflected, speaking at the annual meeting of Randolph Area Community Development Corp.

In fact, it has been difficult to find out just how many homes were destroyed or badly damaged. The best information that *The Herald* has been able to obtain is from a survey of town clerks and other officials performed for Central Vermont Community Action Council. (CVCAC).

The results of that survey were made available by Carol Flint of the Randolph office and produced an estimate of at least 98 homes from which people were displaced because the homes were either totally destroyed or temporarily unusable.

The White River Valley towns with the most destroyed homes were Bethel and Stockbridge, both with 18, and Royalton, with 17. (All numbers remain rough estimates.) Randolph, the biggest town in the Valley, suffered a lot of flooded basements and three displaced businesses, but no destroyed houses, that survey showed. In addition, the towns in the eastern part of the

region—Chelsea, Tunbridge, and Strafford—were spared the loss of homes. So was the town of Brookfield.

In addition to those whose homes were wrecked by the flood, there are others who still cannot reach their homes by car or truck and may not be able to do so for months. As many as 25 families, for instance, live on Stony Brook Road in Stockbridge, and may not have road access for a long time.

'Unfolding' Problem

The housing problem, Carol Flint noted, "is still unfolding."

Communities have done an "amazing job" in the initial emergency response, but fixing the housing problem "is an 18-24-month project," she said. It's a crisis, she noted, that disproportionately affects low income people, who have responded in many different ways.

Families are doubling and tripling up, but that leads to stress, which leads to more substance abuse and domestic violence issues, she pointed out.

The emergency "puts a magnifying glass on the issues that were already here," she notes.

White River: Upper Branch

Rochester

Student volunteers from Middlebury College's Nordic Ski Team take a break from the clean-up to pose with homeowners Tim and Mary Sue Crowley.

"The damage to the ecosystem is so severe that a lot of the animals are going to be in trouble this winter and for a long time."

Tony Korda

Another World Heard From: The Route 100 Valley News from Isolated Towns, *September 8*

Martha Slater

North of Rochester

As I head north from Rochester, I'm surrounded by indisputable testimony to the power of water. I go by my home on Main Street in Rochester village and head north past the Graham-Frock home that washed into the brook, and the Meagher home next door, armored with sandbags.

Across the street lie the ruins of several other homes. Next door to them, a crew of employees at Advanced illumination is busy moving items from the damaged building to take to the company's new location at the former Oatmeal Studios building on State Garage Road.

Up the road, several vehicles are parked by the large old Crowley home, which had been surrounded and invaded by flood waters. Crews of volunteers have been busy there all week, helping the family removed debris and gut the first floor. As I pass the Martin Flats area, where water often comes over the road in heavy rain, I'm surprised to see how comparatively little damage there is to the roadbed there.

Reaching Hancock, I pull in at the Valley Rescue Squad building when I see Danial Sargeant and EMT Tony Korda out front.

An animal lover, Korda tells me that the saddest thing he had seen during the past week was a bloated doe next to the road, drowned while trying to swim for her life.

"The damage to the ecosystem is so severe that a lot of the animals are going to be in trouble this winter and for a long time," he says.

At the Hancock firehouse, the trucks are parked out front, and several volunteers are busy inside making sandwiches. In the aftermath of the storm, the building served as a shelter and, since it has a generator, also provided hot meals and showers for anyone who wanted them.

School board members Rose Juliano praises the efforts of Neil Gibbs, who had stepped up to coordinate emergency services for the town. The other coordinators are Renee Tracy and Jacques Veilleux, who have been at the shelter "almost 24/7." They intend to hold their wedding, as planned, this Saturday, Sept. 10 on the lawn of the Richard Veilleux home on Tunnel Brook Road. Bright pink notices posted around town say the couple will be married then "come Hell or high water."

"We fed an average of 70-80 people at our meals and many stripped their homes to supply the firehouse with refrigerators and other things that were needed."

Gibbs also noted that after the failure of the Fassett Hill Bridge on Route 125 two days before, the state had brought in a temporary one to place over the old one, and it should be in service by the end of the week.

Storm Irene destroyed the bridge on Route 100 that connects Hancock to Rochester.

HANCOCK - GRANVILLE

Weathering the Storm

With 80 miles of Vermont track needing attention in the wake of Irene, New England Central has sub-contracted skilled railroad repair help from all over the country. Donald Lather, Victor Blusk, Jess Lott, Chris Riner, and Richard Tueckhardt came from Maryland and Georgia to repair washouts, restore railroad beds and track. Their companies, Crane Masters and Utilco, seldom work in New England. "We've never been this far north," said one of the crew, adding, "We're 1,300 miles from home and have been working flat out for more than two weeks. Vermont was hit hard."

Keith Currier has lived with his family in a small section of East Granville called "the island" for over two decades. Irene brought a wall of water through this small group of six homes, leaving one condemned. Currier and his daughters Nicole and Angela, with the help of many volunteers, are stripping their entire first floor to the walls in an effort to rebuild.

GRANVILLE

Back at Valley Rescue, Sargeant tells me he had to put off the grand opening of his new Granville General Store.

He tells me that his mother Cheryl, who serves as chair of the town selectboard, had run a shelter at the town hall building last week. Five people slept there on the night of the storm. Residents brought food from their refrigerators and freezers to put in the kitchen there, since there was a generator to keep things running.

"East Granville was hard hit, too. On Tuesday night, I slept in my car about a mile south of Roxbury village, and Wednesday morning, I hiked the 10 miles into East Granville. I found four houses there that had water running through them during the storm. On Thursday, I brought them some food and supplies. As of now, all of the town roads are basically passable."

Postcards from East Granville, *September 22*

One day before Irene, Pheylan Martin (left) headed from East Granville to UVM for his freshman year. "Everything's changed," he said, visiting with his dad, Chris, and neighbor Skip Bent, who were taking a break from restoring Bill Culver's garden plot. "I went into Randolph early in the storm to get supplies with Chris and my wife, Marsha," observed Bent. "The truck was pushing water up to the hood for the last bit on the way home; pretty close to floating." Martin added, "I kept my window open all the way."

Moving oxygen back into the home where he and his mother live, Jeff Lumbra estimates he has worked 275 hours in recovery in the 20 days since the storm. "I was in the house when the railroad embankment failed and saw the wall of water rip right down through our homes. It'll be a long haul before we get this situation right again, but we'll do it."

Extensive flooding shifted the railroad bridge and damaged the abutment in Roxbury, just north of the East Granville town line. Extensive repair by Osmose Railroad Service of Madison, Wisconsin, caused continued closure of Route 12A this week. Residents of East Granville driving to their town clerk's office are now forced to travel south through Braintree and Randolph into Bethel, over Camp Brook Road to Rochester, and then north through Hancock. While this journey of over 30 miles is a great distance, when the road north to Roxbury is open, it's still a trip of more than 20 miles!

> *Down the road,*
> *Sue Flewelling*
> *is on guard at*
> *the cemetery.*

A road crew worker rides in the front of a bucket loader to assess the extent of flooding in Rochester.

ROCHESTER

News from Isolated Towns Continued, *September 8*

Martha Slater

It's the morning of Tuesday, September 6 and I haven't left the village of Rochester for 11 days. As I set out in my little Subaru, heading south on Route 100 to see and report on the clean-up effort after Hurricane Irene, I pass the school where many people in town worked hard to help their fellow residents, and many others found help. Down the road, Sue Flewelling is on guard at the cemetery and work is being done there to repair the section that was washed out.

Parking lots have sprung up next to the road on either side of the demolished bridge onto Route 73, and as I pass, a man is crossing the temporary footbridge to what's been dubbed "the island," toting a big package of toilet paper under one arm.

In some places, the familiar landscape I've always known looks untouched, yet in others it's utterly changed. Water still sluices over the road in some spots and there is mud around every bend. Wide swaths of corn are flattened in some fields, while others still stand upright, their tassels waving in the breeze.

Farms Feel the Hurt from Flood Waters

Liberty Hill Farm's Beth Kennett, comforted by close friend and farm volunteer Lois Bond, walks across some of the 135 acres of feed corn destroyed by Irene's flooding.

Volunteer Asa Manning tries unsuccessfully to burn Liberty Hill's ruined corn crop.

Kennett Cows Swim To Safety, *September 8*

Josey Hastings

The milk truck made its first post-Irene pick-up at Liberty Hill Farm in Rochester on September 3, six days after the storm. According to Beth Kennett, who runs the farm with her husband Bob and her two sons, David and Tom, it was amazing that the truck was able to reach them at all.

It is also amazing that they had any cows to milk. Their herd of 100 milkers was nearly lost in Sunday's floods as waters rose and began to fill the barn where their cows were sheltered.

Realizing they needed to get their herd to higher ground, Tom and David Kennett began moving cows out of the barn, wading through water past their knees. In less than 20 minutes, the water had risen up to their chests, and soon they could no longer touch bottom.

Both men and cows were swimming as they hurried to move the last animals out of the barn. They successfully rescued all 100 cows from drowning.

"Tom, David, and the cows all got swimming lessons," remarked Beth who, as we talked, watched some of the rescued cows grazing on the high ground of her front lawn.

Two women, Carol McLoughlin and Carol Twitchell, saved the Kennett's 30 heifers, their future generation of milkers, which were trapped in a barn north of Rochester. The Kennetts were cut off from the heifer barn by roads that had already become impassable, so McLoughlin and Twitchell waded through flood waters to open the heavy metal gates and push the heifers out of the barn. McLoughlin commented on the rising waters, "I didn't realize how short-legged we were!"

The Kennett Farm can be seen on the bank of the White River, which swelled and damaged a portion of their crops and swept away some cows

Bottom photo: Bob Kennett scoops up a handful of the up to two feet of silt on top of his farm's cornfield.

Second Flood

After the flood of water, a flood of people arrived at Liberty Hill Farm, which had lost all road access. They came on foot, on bike, and on ATVs over mountain roads and paths. A crew of four soldiers rolled up in a Humvee, a group of 10 Vermont Technical College students appeared armed with shovels, six people from the Cabot Creamery Cooperative came from Montpelier, arriving at 10 p.m. on four-wheelers, and a woman and her young son, who the Kennetts had never met before, started coming every day after work to help shovel the barn and feed the cows.

John Curr, the Kennett's IBA dairy supplies salesman, heard that the Kennett's dryer was broken and their flood-sodden work clothes were piling up. He found a way to deliver a new dryer as well as vaccines for the cows, who were at risk of developing respiratory problems as a result of their swim to safety.

"He's helping to keep us healthy and well," said Beth Kennett.

According to Kennett, the Forest Service roads were of vital importance in the week following Irene.

"This network of old roads through the woods served as lines of transportation and communication," she said. "The outside world has expressed their love and concern and our response is 'Thank you, thank you, thank you.' It is a wonderful outpouring of generosity and graciousness."

The Kennetts' field land, corn crops, and haylage were all flooded.

"This coming year's feed is all lost," Kennett commented. "It will be extremely difficult, because we lost the crops in the fields, as well as what we had already harvested." Like many others, the Kennetts' fields are covered in sand and gravel.

"You can't just plant more hay," said Kennett. "It's not that simple. It will take years to recover, because the field land is in really bad shape."

In spite of their losses, Beth Kennett's spirits were high. "We have so much to be thankful for," she said. "We have all of our people and all of our cows. We're alive. We can work. And we're farmers. We know how to work."

A Holstien crosses rough terrain where corn stood seven feet high just weeks ago.

"We have so much to be grateful for. We're alive. We can work. And we're farmers."
Beth Kennett

Report from "Rochester Island"

Letter to the Editor, *September 8*

When Irene's floodwaters collapsed the bridge that connects Route 73 to Route 100, residents in the western (Route 73) part of town, were left stranded on "Rochester Island."

Ginny Sedgwick, West Rochester

I live in West Rochester, (the Rt. 73 portion of Rochester). I'm writing to share with you a personal perspective on what is happening here.

Those of us who live in this section now refer to it as "Rochester Island" because that is what it is now. The bridge that connects Rt. 73 to Rt. 100 collapsed in the flooding. Our community (the village and the island) pulled together and built a walking bridge so we can get into town, but no cars have a way off the island. Rt. 73 to the west is washed out in several areas and reports are that it will be up to three weeks before we'll have access out that way.

Several wealthy part-time residents of the Great Hawk community have chartered private helicopters to take them out of here. Fortunately, for those of us who live here full time, we have enough food and basic necessities to sustain us for a time.

Sadly, some people in our community suffered various levels of loss to their homes – from water damage to complete loss. Our neighbor shared with me the heart-break of helping a family that he is close to shovel mud out of their living room.

I know the complete recovery for our town, as well as several others that have been hit by the flood waters brought by Irene, is going to be long and slow. My husband and I are lucky that our home got through this untouched. My heart goes out to all those who weren't so fortunate.

I'm sending this from my iPhone from the top of the mountain near my home (the only place there is cell service.)

> *I'm sending this from my iPhone from the top of the mountain near my home (the only place there is cell service.)*

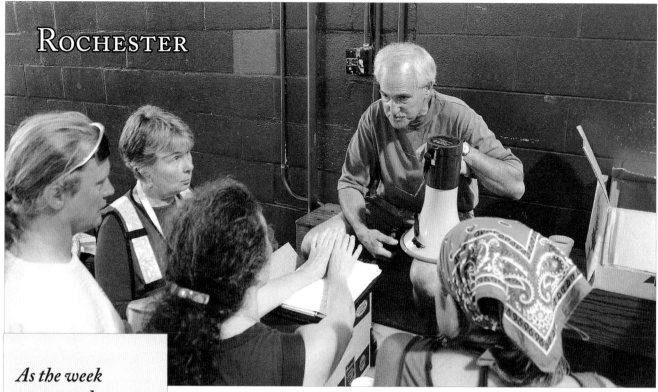

> *As the week progressed, Selectboard Chair Larry Straus' voice began to fade from exhaustion.*

Select Board head Larry Straus answers questions during a town information meeting.

The Little Town That Could (& Did), *September 8*

Martha Slater

The town of Rochester, where my ancestors settled in 1843 and where I've lived for the past 26 years, took a terrible hit from Hurricane Irene last week, but although we may be down, we're not out.

Awful things happened to many people in our town and the valley community north and south of us, but the people have pulled together to help each other out in astonishing and heartwarming ways.

A young woman working at the Skip Mart on Main Street summed it up well when she told me, "I always used to think I lived in a good town with good people, but now I know I do."

Blythe Goupee Bates, who grew up in Rochester and moved back to town with her husband the day before the hurricane struck, said "There's no place I'd rather be than in Rochester. The community is why we're here."

Working Together

Following the storm, daily town meetings to disseminate information about services were held through Sunday, September 4, first at the Federated Church, and then at the school when the shelter was set up there. As the week progressed, Selectboard Chair Larry Straus' voice began to fade from exhaustion, and a bullhorn was produced.

Becky Donnet became the town's acting "food czar," organizing the preparation and serving of three meals a day in the school gym with the school's hot lunch chief, Kristi Fuller, and a loyal crew of volunteers, including several local chefs, who came to help. Donnet also oversaw an informal food shelf at one end of the gym, neatly organized and stocked with a large quantity of donations from all over, and arranged to get supplies that were needed.

Utility crews reset telephone poles on Rte 100 near the junction of Route 73 and a temporary power station for Rochester was installed by CVPS.

Help Arrives

Operating the shelter was made somewhat easier when crews from CVPS, and other linemen, who came from all over, managed to get into town Wednesday afternoon when Route 100 south of the intersection with Route 125 in Hancock, as well as the rest of Route 125 to Middlebury, was made passable. The Rochester substation had been destroyed in the flood and a temporary one was brought from Rutland and put in place.

Leslie Carlson acted as the volunteer "communications czar," coordinating efforts to get people in touch with the outside world. Mail started coming into the Rochester Post Office on Thursday. With over 100 men working 18 hours a day, electrical power was restored to most of Rochester Thursday night and phone service to the outside world was once more available. Repairs were made so that service from the cell tower in the steeple of the Federated Church was also working again.

When Tom Harty of Day's Funeral Home was able to get into town from Randolph on an ATV, he was assisted by several local volunteers in the difficult task of dealing with caskets and remains that had been dislodged from the cemetery south of town. The town's cemetery commissioner Sue Flewelling, also a volunteer, spent many hours guarding the cemetery from sightseers.

Townspeople from both sides of the bridge brought lumber, plywood, nails, and tools to construct a footbridge river to ford the river.

On the 'Island'

"We lucked out by having a lot of excellent machinery and operators on the 'island' side of the bridge, including ECS Excavating, Mac McGuffin and Son, Marc Bowen Excavating, and all the others who worked with them," said one resident.

"They were at it before the state even got there. We wouldn't have been able to save Lyons Bridge or have the roads that they built from nothing on Route 73 toward Brandon, without them."

"The floodwater stopped at row I."
Geoff Olliver

Thea Boardman, 9, of Rochester, waves goodbye to a helicopter contracted by Longtrail Ale to drop off water, food, diapers and baby formula. Long Trail President and CEO, Brian Walsh was on site to help assist the unloading process and talk to community members about what else he and his company could do to help.

The Kindness of Strangers
Help Came from Everywhere, *September 8*

Martha Slater

In addition to all of the tales of local folks who banded together to help each other, there are many stories of the help received through the kindness of strangers. Here are just a few of them.

Among the individuals who helped were Geoff and Patsy Olliver from Queensland, Australia, who were in the U.S. taking a cross-country bicycle trip. They had planned to come through Rochester anyway, and after arriving in the wake of the line trucks, they came to the school to offer their services. After helping remove mud from the auditorium one day, Geoff shook his head in amazement as he told me that night at supper that "the (flood) water stopped at row I!"

Many donations of food and supplies for the meals at the shelter and the food shelf there came from groups, but innumerable others came from individuals.

One example was a couple who arrived Sunday afternoon in an SUV packed full of items they had purchased at Costco in Burlington. The man told me he made sure to get "juice boxes and cereal for the kids."

While musician Jerry Shedd is certainly no stranger to Rochester, having come here to perform many times, he makes his home in Middlebury. He also arrived on Sunday after a circuitous trip, with dairy products and other needed items.

Rochester resident Cynthia Fowles was out of town at the time of the storm and it took her three days to get back into the valley, but she used them traveling around to collect donations from many businesses.

> "*I have seen more pain, heartbreak, and devastation than I ever thought I'd see in my lifetime.*"
> **Governor Peter Shumlin**

A soldier replaces the blade on his chainsaw while working in the Route 100 valley.

In Rochester, Governor Cites 'Extraordinary Acts,' *September 15*

Martha Slater

Governor Peter Shumlin re-visited Rochester Wednesday afternoon, Sept. 7, just one week after his initial trip here following the disastrous flooding caused by Hurricane Irene.

After making a stop at the Rochester Café to speak with owners Tim and Sue Domas and café patrons, the governor and several staffers,

along with Phil Fiermonte, outreach director for Senator Bernie Sanders, met with Rochester residents on the corner of the village park.

Rain fell and trucks rumbled by, going back and forth from repair work on Bethel Mountain Road, occasionally drowning out the governor's voice as he gave an update on progress made in the past week.

"We are where we are because of extraordinary acts by Vermonters," he said.

"We have made incredible progress. There were 72,000 Vermonters without power last week, and after the hard work of so many crews, there are now only 47 left who don't have power."

Shumlin also praised the quick work of President Obama in granting approval of individual assistance.

"He turned all that paperwork around in less than two hours on Sunday," he said.

The governor reminded everyone to call FEMA at 1-800-621-3212 if they needed to file disaster assistance paperwork, and also noted that the state had set up a program to grant extremely low-interest loans of up to $100,000 to Vermont businesses that suffered from the flood.

On the subject of removing gravel from rivers to help prevent future flooding, Governor Shumlin said, "We washed the red tape for that down the river with John's house," referring to John Graham, whose house on the south end of the village had been destroyed. "We can get that gravel out now."

"This is a tough time for so many," he said. "I have seen more pain, heartbreak, and devastation than I ever thought I'd see in my lifetime. We're getting through it because of our spirit, but now people are getting tired. Watch out for your neighbors who are struggling. It's not a sign of weakness to have some help from a counselor now that the adrenaline is gone."

Asked about the timeline for replacing the bridge onto Route 73, the governor noted that he had brought in over 300 engineers from all over to inspect and assess the many bridges around the state that were damaged or destroyed, and was expecting a report from them within a few days, "and your bridge is high up on the list."

Winding it up, the governor said "I'm proud of all of you," and he led a round of applause for the efforts of

Selectboard Chair Larry Straus and other town officials and volunteers.

Heading south out of town, Governor Shumlin made a visit to the "island" community on Route 73, walking across the footbridge that is the only way to get there from town. He met with residents there on the front porch of the former Rochester Electric building.

There was praise and a round of applause for the hard work of Dave and Betty Chase in helping their neighbors in the Route 73 community since the storm.

"We washed the red tape for that down the river with John's house. We can get that gravel out now."

Damaged equipment at White River Golf Course.

White River Golf Course Suffers Severe Damage from Hurricane, *September 29*

Martha Slater

Most of the White River Golf Course, which is the largest business in Rochester (in terms of land mass, since it occupies 50 acres of real estate), was under nine feet of water at the height of the flooding caused by Hurricane Irene.

"The course was devastated," reported Alan Moore. "A thick layer of silt covered many fairways, and trees were uprooted or wrapped with debris from upriver. The clubhouse basement was completely flooded and tenants in the two apartments on the second floor have had no running water since then—one family has two small children."

Moore added that the barn housing the mowing equipment was flooded, so "each machine has been compromised with silt and must be stripped down, cleaned and reassembled before any chance that it can run. Fire crews from Middlebury, Vergennes and Bristol helped in the early stages to clean out the basement, and more recently, a kind-hearted soul from Ferrisburgh donated time and machinery to help clear silt, damaged trees and other detritus. A few valley residents have found time to help pick stones from fairways and cut up wood with chainsaws. A small core of volunteers have attended daily to chip away at what is a Herculean task."

Moore said that "People assume golf courses all make money hand over fist, but that's not so. Owner and operator, Peter McGowan pays $14,000 per annum in local taxes and hosts the annual tournament to benefit the Park House. It attracts second-home owners who buy gas and use the grocery store and eateries in town. Vermont residents also come from Waitsfield, Warren, Bethel, South Royalton and further afield to play here. If this local business were to go under, then the effect would undeniably be felt in Rochester.

> *"People assume golf courses all make money hand over fist, but that's not so."*
> *Alan Moore*

Heavy equipment operator Dave Colton of Pittsfield worked long hours with several others to clear a path from the north to the south side of town after Irene destroyed three bridges, leaving Pittsfield isolated from the outside world.

> *The town lost nine homes to catastrophic damage and at least 20 suffered severe damage.*

Tweed River

PITTSFIELD

A Tour of Isolated Towns, Continued, *September 8*

Martha Slater

Further south on Route 100, the bridge at Guernsey Hollow, near the Colton Farm, has washed away, but the road continues with a one-lane dirt track that swoops down and then up again like a roller coaster, and is marked "residents only." Past that, all the way into Pittsfield village, signs caution "15 m.p.h."

At her office next to the green, Town Clerk Patty Haskins calls the town's emergency management coordinator Peter Borden on his cell phone, and arranges for me to go to the intersection of Route 100 and Lower Michigan Road to speak with him at the site of yet another bridge that was washed out. There I find that it wasn't only the bridge—the road itself was heavily damaged and soldiers from the Army Corps of Engineers are hard at work, maneuvering heavy equipment. Several homes on the left-hand side of the road are obviously destroyed.

"Our whole town has put in long days, but, I've gotten a couple of hours of sleep every night," Borden says. "Right now, we're doing nothing but hazard mitigation."

"The town lost nine homes to catastrophic damage, and at least 20 suffered severe damage," he adds, as a huge caterpillar-treaded backhoe creaks and rumbles by. "75% of our culverts washed out, but as of now, all of our town roads are passable."

Tracy Templeton of Pittsfield holds a sign that says it all.

Families sat on the drying grass enjoying steak, burgers, sausages, grilled pizza, salads and breads.

It Was the Wrong/Right Time To Visit Pittsfield! Part 2, *October 27*

Candace Leslie

Meantime, the Clear River Inn, south of the village, turned bad luck into a festival. Lacking large generators, the staff hauled their vast amounts of perishable food up to the town's green and hosted a huge noon-time barbecue for several hundred folks. Families sat on the drying grass enjoying steak, burgers, sausages, grilled pizza, salads and breads. Youngsters with wagons roamed the crowd, offering up hundreds of pints of beginning-to-melt Ben and Jerry's ice cream from the Pitt Stop. No one bothered to enforce the open container law—just this once.

I attended town meetings with Karen at 7:30 several mornings. Here I was even more overwhelmed by the tremendous ability of the townsfolk for meeting each other's needs and for action wherever it was called for. The meetings were exceptionally well organized. After reports were made on the state of things each particular day, individuals continued offering more ways to help. People knew where seniors on oxygen might need a generator for a few hours, and saw to it that they got them. Roger sold gasoline for a designated hour each morning and afternoon—only for working ATVs and generators. The spirit that permeated the church's packed sanctuary (the largest gathering place in the village) was breathtaking. I felt it a gift to be among these amazing Vermonters.

Later Karen would tell me, "I have always loved Pittsfield. Now I also feel very proud."

Near top photos: On the heels of Tropical Storm Irene, Monday, August 29, Pittsfield residents began to organize themselves in daily morning meetings at the Federated Church with Selectman George Deblon as moderator.

Ellen Martin (on left), whose Pittsfield village home served as the town's Information Clearinghouse, and Town Clerk Patricia Haskins (on right).

Helicopters were bringing in "Ready Meals" and bottled water.

On Friday the power had come back on. Helicopters were bringing in "Ready Meals" and bottled water. We learned we could get away the next morning during a one-hour window open to a long line of waiting traffic. (If you did choose to leave, it was with the understanding you would not be allowed back. Other than that one hour, the roads would be open only to road repair machinery.) We would need to be at Killington by 8 a.m., which meant leaving Pittsfield at seven for the drive that normally took 20 minutes. So after supper we packed up and said our goodbyes to Karen, and to Bruce and Colby who had managed, with much

chutzpah and scheming, to get in earlier that morning. At least Karen would not be lonely for a while. Still, she came over at 6 a.m. on Saturday with bananas, bottles of water, and a last goodbye.

As we turned out of the Lower Michigan Road onto ravaged Route 100, I took a last look at a house that was leaning precariously into the river. Someone had sprayed big letters on the outer wall. They spelled out: "IRENE YOU BITCH."

We left behind an isolated village, a phenomenal community, hundreds of miles of destroyed highways, and, the next day, the state of Vermont, all of which would be long in recovering from

> *We left behind an isolated village, a phenomenal community, which would be long in recovering from "the bitch."*

"the bitch." There would be no lucrative autumn foliage tourism, and perhaps not even a good ski season. Thousands of crops were ruined. Homes, covered bridges, and several town centers were wiped out. Fortunately, there was almost no loss of life.

Glad as I was to be going home, I knew I would miss Pittsfield for a long time.

[Editor's Note: An inspirational slide show, called "Pittsfield Proud" by Barb Wood is posted on YouTube.]

Stockbridge neighbors organize on Monday, August 29, to rebuild their community's washed out roads.

A Tour of Isolated Towns Continued, *September 8*

Martha Slater

Nearing Stockbridge, I see sections of guardrail that separate from the road like the peel on a banana. Chunks of the roadside are gone, and several homes have huge piles of household debris filling their front yards.

After making the right turn at Ted Green Ford, I discover that while the new bridge survived, the pavement on the northern approach to it has crumpled like aluminum foil, leaving just one lane open.

Just past the intersection with Route 107, I pull into the parking lot for the Stockbridge Town Clerk's Office and the post office.

There I find Barb Green and Stephanie Colton sorting through mounds of muddy office equipment and soggy cardboard boxes in front of the town building.

They tell me that Colton's sister, Town Clerk Cathy Brown, has set up temporary quarters across the street at the Teeny Tozier's restaurant, which isn't open during the summer. Green assures me that her family's business survived just fine, and Colton, a teacher at the Stockbridge Central School, says she hopes school will be able to open soon.

Inside the town office, Colton shows me the marks on the wall where student artwork from the school was displayed and explains that it was saved from damage. Interior walls are gutted to the studs. At the neighboring post office, the front door is propped open to dry out the muddy interior and the building is deserted.

Crossing Route 100, I make my way into the restaurant building, past tables and countertops covered with papers and other items from the town office. I find Brown in the back, talking on the phone with a resident who has questions. Later she tells me that about half of the town records in the vault suffered damage and have been sent to Massachusetts, where they will be frozen and restored.

> *The pavement on the northern approach to it has crumpled like aluminum foil.*

Bill Johnson and his son Greg, 12, carry fuel into neighbors working on River Road.

STOCKBRIDGE

Major Roadblock: Route 107 Still Closed, Mangled East-West Artery May Open for Residents, *September 15*

M. D. Drysdale

The good news from Route 107 west of Bethel is that a huge contingent of engineers and heavy equipment operators have constructed a new roadbed for the section where the state route simply disappeared.

The bad news is that later rains destabilized the banks above the new roadbed, sending mud and even trees across it.

As a result, the Department of Transportation (VTrans) has put the road off-limits even to local people whose homes are on the wrong side of the washout. They hope that local traffic can be restored by the end of the week—but only at night, leaving the daylight hours free for construction equipment.

No state highway in the White River Valley suffered more horrendous damage from Irene than Route 107, which is the main east-west corridor from Route 100 and points west.

The closure of Route 107 effectively cut off the towns of Stockbridge, Pittsfield, and Rochester from their usual commute to Bethel. And since U.S. Route 4 from Route 100 to Woodstock was also destroyed, east-west transportation became almost impossible.

In particular, the 1.5-mile section between Tozier's Restaurant and Lambert's Chainsaw Repair was totally wiped out—not just the road surface but the entire structure of the roadway. Observers said that it gave the impression that a road had never been built there—just a river.

Like Magic

"The road just disappeared," a state official said. "David Copperfield would have been proud."

A semblance of a roadway was put back in place, enough to allow local residents to reach their homes for

about three days. But after recent rains, which caused trees to collapse into the construction area, VTrans closed the 1.5-mile segment totally on Tuesday, except for emergency vehicles.

With luck, VTrans said, local traffic may be able to start using that road—during the nighttime only—by the end of this week.

"Restoring access to Route 107 is a state priority," a release from VTrans said. "Crews are working diligently to repair the road, stabilize the embankment and clear trees that are in danger of falling into the roadway.

"Although crews are allowing emergency vehicles to traverse the roadway if necessary, the area is not safe for public use and remains closed to all personal vehicles."

Bottom photo: Michael Hanson, left, and Gregory Bakos of Vanasse Hangen Brustlin, Inc. talk while walking along the temporary road where Route 107 once ran. Their company designed the replacement.

The loss of the bridge across the Third Branch at Riford Brook, combined with road destruction about two miles up the valley, has isolated the community of about seventy from the outside world.

Julia Hutchinson and Bart Parmelee work with Jake Mann and Carrie Baker to pull over 1,000 pounds of frozen pork, chicken and beef across the chasm at Riford Brook Bridge, Tuesday, August 30. It is estimated that more than one hundred people were isolated on Riford Brook and Thayer Brook Roads by road and bridge destruction.

THIRD BRANCH

RIFORD BROOK

Thirty-six members of Braintree's isolated Riford Brook Road neighborhood gathered for an emergency meeting at Mike and Linda Gaidys home, Tuesday morning, August 30.

Having finally reached safe terrain, a small convoy of ATVs manages to navigate a route out of Riford Brook on Monday afternoon. At their August 30 meeting, the community elected to seek, build, and blaze a safer ATV route, knowing that it would be days before roads would be open.

Julia Hutchinson, using mountaineering equipment, hauls up one portion of the frozen food. The huge cavity below has exposed the I-beam sub-structure, rendering the bridge a total loss.

Celeste and Bud Grant's place is under water, and Celeste, with medical complications, needed hospitalization. Their son Rick and his wife Sherry tried to get them out Sunday evening, but the water was too strong and the bridge was failing.

WEST BRAINTREE

Disaster Strengthens Community Ties
Reflections While Walking into West Braintree
September 1

Bob Eddy

In West Braintree last Monday evening, the only sound was of water spilling in cataracts over broken asphalt and across rock-littered front yards.

I visited the village of West Braintree on Monday evening. The way in is a walk along the railroad bed. Perhaps 20 folks were coming and going as I started out.

To someone passing through in a car, this hamlet is little more than a blink of country homes. On foot, the community reveals itself.

The Maxhams and Whites are walking out, on their way to Randolph for supplies as I start up the tracks. Their homes are OK, compared with many others.

Celeste and Bud Grant's place is under water, and Celeste, with medical complications, needed hospitalization. Their son Rick and his wife Sherry tried to get them out Sunday evening, but the water was too strong and the bridge was failing. They spent the night on higher ground at Jeff Vinton's Thunder Mountain Farm and were evacuated by the Randolph Center Fire Department on Monday morning.

Pam White's parting words were, "If you write about this, could you let folks know my day care will be closed until further notice?"

I don't know Bud and Celeste, but Sherry works with Mary Merusi at Beacon Printing. Mary's home is here, too, just visible through brush along the tracks. Stuart's sugarhouse used to be down here across the tracks from the home. All that's left is a concrete slab, scoured bare by the flood.

Two young folks join me in my walk. Nathan Cleveland, introduces himself and I wonder aloud if he was related to the Clevelands in Peth. "Yes, Sherry Grant is my aunt." (Then I remembered that Sherry was a Cleveland before she was a Grant.)

"Jesse Ernst is also my cousin." Jesse and his young family are my Braintree Hill neighbors. Connections are being made.

"I'm Izzy Young," smiled our other traveler. Her grandparents are Charlie and Shirley Young of Bethel Gilead. My thoughts range back 35 years and I see Shirley working the cash register next to Francis Chase at Central Supplies, and Charlie plowing us out on Mountain Avenue.

Together we walk into the village. The only sound is of water running, spilling in cataracts over broken

Luke and Cindy Rose walk supplies in to Luke's pregnant wife Kate in West Braintree, Monday evening, August 29.

Our cars and TVs, computers and radios have made the world smaller, but they have also diminished it.

asphalt and down across rock littered front yards. Here is Celeste and Bud's home, still surrounded by a pond. The front steps float free like a raft, strange because they seem so right out there in the middle of the water.

I recognize Duane King's place. We purchased Ruby, our golden retriever, from Duane's daughter Marcy two years ago. Her home is up in back. It still stands, and I quietly hope that they are all spared much damage. I am walking in the middle of a very quiet, empty, state highway.

I knock at Mary Merusi's door, just to wish her well. She's not in, but evidence of her battle with flood and mud is everywhere. Strangely, mercifully, a small pond is draining quickly down a hole in the middle of her back yard.

Back on the tracks there are many people coming and going. Jeff Potwin and his family walk back to their car after an unsuccessful effort to get word from family up in Roxbury. Brothers George and Jeff Smith pass on their way to see how their mother is doing.

Gil Rose negotiates his way with supplies on a dirt bike, followed by his wife Cindy and son Luke on foot with more supplies. Luke's wife Kate is almost full-term. The logistics of her late-stage pregnancy have been complicated in myriad ways.

Walt Palmer has stopped for a breather on the trestle bridge. I last saw him 26 hours ago, inspecting damage on Braintree Hill. A Braintree selectman and road foreman, he's headed home to bed after working for 36 hours straight.

"Randolph has established access up Thayer Brook Road," he tells me, adding, "We're headed up to Howard's mill first thing in the morning. That road's the only way folks on top and all the way down Riford Brook are going to get out."

Further on I stop at Verlie Farnsworth's. The last time I was here was over two decades ago. We sit for a few minutes, reflect upon the day, share news.

At the car, I realize my walk into West Braintree has afforded conversation and sharing impossible driving through at 30 miles an hour. Our cars and TVs, computers and radios have made the world smaller, but they have also diminished it. Everywhere the road surfaces end and cars are left behind, Vermonters are walking, visiting and banding together. We are sharing stories and food, blankets, generators, water and shelter. Roads, electricity and phones may be down, but folks in isolated hills and valleys are building stronger community with each conversation, with each act of good will.

Braintree School Is Rolling;
Commute Can Be Rough, *September 22*

Sandy Vondrasek

This is how Janni Jacobs used to get to work: Climb in her Honda Civic and make the 10-minute or so drive to Braintree Elementary School, where she teaches students grades 4-6.

This is how Jacobs, who lives on Riford Brook Road in Braintree, makes the trip to school now:

First, just to get from her home to Riford Brook Road, she crosses two makeshift footbridges— one made of logs, the other planks—over Riford Brook.

(Flash-flooding on August 28, she explained, turned the brook into a 40-foot wide torrent that ripped away her small driveway bridge. The brook has since subsided, but now runs in two parallel streams in the widened channel.)

Jacobs then hikes a mile down the road to the blown-out end of Riford Brook Road bridge and clambers down into the chasm created when flood waters ripped out the western approach to the bridge.

She climbs up the two ladders strapped onto the exposed cement abutment, retrieves her bicycle from Ron and Kim Connolly's garage ("I never had a garage before," she says with a smile), and bikes the half-mile north on Route 12A to the school.

Her 30-minute morning commute has been a little frosty, some days, but Jacobs says she is enjoying the morning ritual.

> *She climbs up the two ladders strapped onto the exposed cement abutment, retrieves her bicycle from Ron and Kim Connolly's garage, and bikes the half-mile north on Route 12A to the school.*

Janni Jacobs used to commute to work in her Honda. It took about five minutes. Now, taking at least half an hour, she has to ride two separate bikes, one on each side of a tricky ladder-climb to get to the top of the washed out Riford Brook bridge.

For their daily trip to Braintree School, Sam Paddock ferries his grandchildren, Shawn Paddock, and Hayley, Natalie, and Lauren Messier across Riford Brook by tractor and the rest of the way by car. While inconvenient, this mile-and-three-quarter, two-vehicle solution is preferable to 12 miles on rough Thayer Brook Road.

Janni Jacobs climbs up two ladders strapped onto the exposed cement embankment.

> "If you're missing a culvert, almost a dozen have washed up here."
> Donny Wood

Irene Damages Golf Course, But It Still Has Seven Holes, *September 1*

Marjorie Drysdale

Looking over the devastation wreaked upon the Montague Golf Club in Randolph this week, one is tempted to begin spouting out Biblical passages. The saved and the damned. The wheat and the chaff.

Here's why: Half the course is as pristine as ever. The other half is destroyed.

But the spirit of the place is as strong as ever.

"We're open for seven holes, and proud of it," declared Paul Meunier, PGA professional golf director at Montague.

"We may not have power, but we have energy," exclaimed another worker as he jumped into a cart. Club House Manager Cathy Stroutsos invited me into another cart and proceeded to give me a tour.

The upper course is as picturesque as ever, with long expanses of green, manicured lawns dotted by tall, whispering pines. Some people were out and about, enjoying a game.

But when we reached the brink of the plateau, we saw a moonscape, with this difference: Instead of barren rock, there were thousands of ridges of gray silt, undulating in random and dizzying patterns. Their course was interrupted by downed trees, exposed pipes and wires, and the detritus of the hopes and dreams of scores of people upstream.

"We found an entire sports shed," said Stroutsos, "filled with things like volleyballs and nets."

"If you're missing a culvert, almost a dozen have washed up here," added Donny Wood. Some of them look brand-new.

Taking a glance downstream myself, I noticed a huge pile of new lumber. Somebody must have been planning to build a house.

For those of you familiar with the course, the tenth green has been washed away. The eighteenth fairway is lost. The driving range is gone. The pump house, still standing in a pool of water, is no longer functional. Nobody knows the severity of the leaks to the irrigation system.

About a dozen people took all day to shovel off the sixth green. Now they are blowing off the silt in an effort to save it. "No oxygen can get to the grass unless we get the silt off," Stroutsos explained.

"When Kimball (a reference to Robert Kimball, who also built Randolph's library at the turn of the last century) first built this course, it had six holes," said Meunier. "Now it does again. Six or seven. At least for now."

Just then, two men from out-of-town walked by. They loved playing on this course. Joe Balzanelli from Arizona had been staying at Abel Mountain Campground in Braintree, owned by Paul Rea.

"First an earthquake and now a flood," Balzanelli quipped. He is now staying with relatives in Berlin, but plans to go back to Arizona soon.

His friend, Lenny Hutchinson of Barre, shook his head in disbelief. The two had just been playing at Montague a week ago. "It's such a shame. They had done such a fantastic job in fixing it up," he said.

Randolph Roads Are Now Fully Passable

September 8

M. D. Drysdale

Randolph roads suffered a severe hit in the flood of 2001, but the town's fate was not as bad as some of its neighbors.

Fast work by the town crew, led by Bill Morgan and Rob Runnals, made all roads passable by the end of the day Tuesday, though permanent repairs will take much longer.

Perhaps the toughest fix was an enormous trench that opened up at the north end of the Brook Street bridge that leads to Lincoln Ave. and other streets in the area that used to be called the Rowell Addition. Residents were never quite cut off—the sidewalk, strangely, stayed intact.

Another severe washout occurred on the Pleasant Street Ext., which also required many truckloads of sand.

The pedestrian bridge at the playground—washed out in the 1970s—will have to be replaced, as it was twisted by the force of the Third Branch.

Back roads mainly fared well, though Howard Hill needed repairs.

A shelter for hurricane victims was set up at Vermont Technical College, through a collaboration between David Sanville of Gifford Medical Center and President Philip Conroy of Vermont Tech. Approximately 20 beds are available. Several people from Bethel used the shelter Sunday night. Those at the shelter will have beds in the college dorm, bathrooms and showers, food, and a coin laundry.

Randolph Rotary Sends 75 Barbecued Chickens to Rochester, *September 8*

Randolph Rotary occupied the center of town this Friday to grill chickens and raise money for community service.

The Labor Day barbecue is an annual event, but there was a difference this year. Rotary honored the road crews and the people of Rochester for their dedication and hard work caused by Hurricane Irene.

Randolph Rotary brought a large number of grilled chickens to Rochester and donated chickens to each of the local road crewmen that came by. The event was co-sponsored by the Randolph National Bank.

David Palmer looks over the guardrail into the chasm left after waters destroyed the bridge on Lincoln Avenue in Randolph. The sidewalk, strangely, stayed intact.

Bethel Town Hall Buzzes With Flood Activity

Sandy Levesque, volunteer coordinator for Bethel's Disaster Clearinghouse, makes an entry on the planning board at the Old Town Hall.

September 15

M. D. Drysdale

On Saturday, September 3, six days after the big flood, the remodeled Bethel Town Hall was pulsing with energy, serving as the headquarters for Bethel relief work.

Dozens of volunteers (including about 30 from South Royalton) turned out and were sent to various locations where there was a need. Coordinating the effort with a white board, constantly being updated, was Sandy Levesque of Bethel Gilead, assisted by several lieutenants.

Upstairs, the entire main hall of the building was full of tables overflowing with donated clothing. Donations poured in not only from Bethel and area towns, but from as far away as Burlington and Maine.

In charge was Crystal Washburn, who had the donations carefully separated by size, gender, etc.

In a separate room was a good supply of personal supplies to replenish flooded-out bathrooms and kitchens. Presiding there was Shannah Young, who grew up in Bethel Gilead but now lives in Boston. Shannah read on Facebook the reports of damage in Bethel and immediately headed north to help.

As the morning wore on, Levesque knew that the volunteers were getting hungry, but she could figure out no way to provide them with lunches. Then, like magic, two strangers appeared, all the way from Hardwick—with a barbecue grill, chili, and lots of hot dogs.

"We have had donations here from every part of Vermont and as far away as Massachusetts."
Paula Beal

Surrounded by clothing donations in the Old Town Hall, Governor Peter Shumlin arrived in Bethel on Sunday, September 4, to hold a People's Forum.

Bottom, Clothing donations quickly piled up at the Disaster Clearinghouse where volunteers like Crystal Washburn, here, sorted and distributed resources to flood victims.

Bethel Food Shelf Expands Hours, *September 8*

Amy Danley-White

The Bethel Food Shelf in the basement of the White Church is usually open only four hours a week. That changed a few days after the flood.

The directors of the food shelf arranged for the food shelf to be open five days a week, from 9 a.m.-5 p.m., until Bethel residents' need for emergency food and cleaning supplies has been met.

Paula Beal, a regular volunteer who has helped in coordinating supplies this past week, said, "We have had donations here from every part of Vermont and as far away as Massachusetts." She said, "The Faith Assembly of God hosted a free dinner for the town on Sunday night, September 4. They served at the White Church 150 meals and sent 50 meals out to those unable to come into town. St. Anthony's Catholic Church will start hosting free dinners from 5-7 p.m. until the need is met."

Beal said, "The men of the church cleaned out a storage section in the basement to take in the cleaning supplies from the town hall." Among the cleaning items donated are disaster cleaning kits from the Red Cross that include, but are not limited to, brooms, a mop, a squeegee, and various cleaning solutions.

> *"Doggonit, they're
> a resilient bunch."*
> Jim Perrin

Bethel Gilead Farm Report, *September 8*

Josey Hastings

Gilead Brook Road in Bethel was severely flooded in the storm. Jim Perrin, a milk tester with the Dairy Herd Improvement Association (DHIA), reported that Derrick and Beverly Wright, who own a dairy farm at the far end of the road were, as of the writing of this article on September 3, still unable to ship milk or receive grain. Their phone lines were also still down, but according to Perrin, the Wrights have a garden, and "it's a good thing they put up a lot of vegetables."

Perrin also reported that the Wrights were working on cutting a trail that would allow them to get through the woods on a 4-wheeler in order to get fuel for their generator to milk the cows.

Although the Wrights have to dump their milk until the milk truck can reach them, their cows still need to be milked to avoid mastitis and other health complications, and to maintain production.

"This means a lot of heartache," said Jim Perrin. "A lot of blood, sweat, and tears go into producing that product, and then you watch it go down the drain. It makes you appreciate the farmers a whole bunch, because doggonit they're a resilient bunch."

Farmers who are unable to receive grain due to washed-out roads will have to reduce grain rations and, as a result, will face reduced milk production. Once milk production goes down for a cow, it is hard, if not impossible, to bring that production back up before the end of the lactation cycle. Therefore, farmers who have to significantly reduce grain rations may see their total milk production compromised over the next several months.

Wayne Townsend, working in Bethel Gilead on Labor Day, said, "I've probably cut and cleared 1,000 trees since the storm so far. Gone through four chains in a week because of all the grit on the wood."

The Charge of the Mighty Mud Brigade

September 8

Kathy Rohloff

Countless stories have been told and will be told in years to come about the effects of Hurricane Irene on Vermont. And they will be tales of heroism, selflessness, acceptance, bravery, generosity, and kindness.

We witnessed the effects of the Mighty Mud Brigade. These were individuals of all ages, from Vermont and surrounding states, with diverse backgrounds. The common ground was their love for Vermont.

Some members used our home on River Road in Bethel as a base camp to wield their skills. We were the designated babysitters and cooks, the suppliers of hot showers, clean towels, and beds.

Over the Labor Day weekend all the mud from the basements of the houses that availed themselves of their labor was cleared. Generally, a crew of 20-30 individuals formed a bucket line. The first into the mud were gloved, masked, and booted shovelers down cellar; the heavy half-filled pails were heaved to the guy "in the hole" who hefted them shoulder high and out the window; the debris was passed from person to person outside and then deposited. School age children would tote the empty buckets back for the process to begin all over again.

A camaraderie developed among the workers. Everyone was soon on a first name basis with their place of residence thrown in. Mike from Long Island. Samantha and Hannah from Boston. Kelly from Connecticut.

But soon others earned their names. "Jersey" was identified by his clothing, "Little Girl" and "Big Guy" by their size. And the gal that spent hours "in the hole" outlasting everyone in endurance and the number of buckets lifted (way over 500 pails) was aptly christened, "The Machine."

And of course, there were the inevitable and oft-repeated mud jokes. Have some liquid goo splash in your face and a comrade would yell, "Just use your glove to wipe it off!" (Said glove was already encrusted with inches of the stuff.) Clean a shovel and need to dry it? "There's a clean dry spot on your back," someone would quip.

Fill the bucket too low and someone "in the hole" would yell, "Hey, we're not feeding horses back here." If there was too much mud in a container, surely it was the other guy's fault for being over-zealous.

Throughout the day donations of sandwiches, homemade cookies, chocolate bars, and bottled water arrived. The generosity was overwhelming.

Meaning no disrespect to Alfred Lord Tennyson, I write: "Into the valley of Bethel marched the Mighty Mud Brigade. Mud to the right of them, mud to the left of them, mud all around them shuddered and trembled. Assailed by heat and dust, boldly they pushed and shoved, moving that nasty mud, the Mighty Mud Brigade.

"Their only quick reply, 'Pass the bucket up the line.' Their only reason why, 'Find the floor, you're doing fine.' Theirs but to shovel and sweat, moving the mud that's wet, the Mighty Mud Brigade.

"When will their glory fade? Never, not in our days. Hats off to you we say. Oh, Mighty Mud Brigade.

Thank you!

> *Theirs but to shovel and sweat, moving the mud that's wet, the Mighty Mud Brigade.*

Three members of the Mighty Mud Brigade: "The Machine," Kelly, and Hannah.

Camp Brook Road

Bethel Selex Discuss Irene, *September 15*

Amy Danley-White

The Bethel Selectboard's meeting September 12 at the Bethel Town Offices was all about efforts to dig out from under the wrath of Hurricane Irene.

Bethel Selectboard Chair Neal Fox commended Town Manager Dell Cloud for being one of the first town managers to talk to FEMA about winter maintenance on flood-damaged roads. Cloud was the fifth town manager in the state to apply for public assistance for their town, Fox said.

Camp Brook Road may be eligible for federal reconstruction aid, because it is listed as a major collector highway. Cloud said no one from the federal highways department has seen or met with him yet, but there is a possibility that federal aid may cover 100% of repair costs.

"There are a lot of ifs and maybes with these promises of reimbursement," Fox cautioned.

"This storm caused much more damage than the flood of 2007," Cloud noted. "We are still paying back Mascoma Bank for what we borrowed back that time," Cloud said.

Cloud announced there is now a large crusher at the Rock of Ages quarry on Christian Hill Road big enough to crush large loads of granite. He said the crusher is under his direction and authority. Dump trucks are going up Christian Hill and leaving the quarry via a new emergency entrance ramp to I-89 South.

Bethel gets mutual aid from Rock of Ages by getting free stone for town road projects. Surrounding towns pay a small fee for crushed material.

> "There are a lot of ifs and maybes with these promises of reimbursement."
> **Neal Fox**

A train drops 15 carloads of large stones onto Peavine Boulevard in Bethel for use as fill in the repairs of Route 107.

STONE BOATS - A convoy of super-sized trucks ferry huge blocks of quarried stone from the landing beside the tracks in Bethel village, across a makeshift ford of the White River, to the new roadbed of flood obliterated Route 107. These three are headed back for more.

Bethel Selex Hold Emergency Meeting Regarding Route 107, *October 6*

Amy Danley-White

The Bethel Selectboard held an emergency meeting Monday, October 3 to discuss how to get large stone for the road base of devastated Route 107.

Mark Colgan, director of Engineering Services for Vanasse, Hagan, Brustlin, Inc., came to the meeting to speak on this issue for the state Agency of Transportation. He said that in order to finish even a partially reconstructed road before Thanksgiving, the contractors needed large stone for foundation for the roadbed.

Colgan said that when flood repair work first started, the engineers counted 33 repair sites on the Bethel portion of Route 107. Of those 33 sites, six were so large—from between 500-2,000 feet long—they were designated as areas, to differentiate them from the other 27 sites. He pointed out that of the six

areas, only three remain for major repair: Area 1 is 2,000 feet long, Area 2 is 500 feet long, and Area 3 is 1,500 feet long.

"Material has been the biggest challenge," Colgan said. "We need 100,000 cubic yards of 4 to 5 foot riprap. On top of that, all over the state people need it. Gravel isn't the issue, rock is."

Colgan said that on Saturday, he met with the New England Central Railroad and the Vermont Railroad to ask if it was possible if trains could deliver stone and drop it off on Peavine Boulevard.

The answer he received was yes. They could send a train with side dumping cars so riprap could be unloaded to roll from the railway down to Peavine Boulevard. They would send one train a day filled with stone from a quarry in Burlington. The railroad told him it would be a 24-hour operation in Burlington to fill, send, and re-fill cars.

> *They would send one train a day filled with stone from a quarry in Burlington.*

Second Branch

BROOKFIELD

Brookfield Farm Report, *September 8*

Josey Hastings

Goats' Milk

Fat Toad Farm, a goat dairy in Brookfield, was fortunate enough to survive the storm with land and animals intact, but they did lose 3200 jars of caramel. The caramel, made from milk from their goats, had been fully packaged and was sitting in a Foundry Park warehouse on Prince Street in Randolph waiting to be shipped. The warehouse, located near a branch of the White River, filled with about three feet of water, submerging the

caramel, as well as $1,500 worth of shipping and packaging materials.

The loss of caramel, which is not covered by insurance, represents about three weeks of milk and labor. "We could ill afford to lose that product," commented Steve Reid, co-owner of Fat Toad Farm, "but when I look around at the damage and loss that others have incurred, I realize that it's peanuts in comparison." The farm will be donating all profits from their online September 7th sales to Evening Song Farm in Cuttingsville, a vegetable CSA that lost their whole farm in the floods.

Operation Revive Royalton Is Ready To Help Flood Victims, *September 1*

Pamela Levasseur

Sarah Buxton, representative for Royalton and Tunbridge, reports that Vermont has been declared a federal disaster area by President Obama and Governor Shumlin.

The Royalton area alone has an estimated $10 million of damage, said Buxton.

For immediate relief, Buxton has organized a volunteer relief effort to help anyone that has been affected by the recent storm and flooding.

Locally, she has been coordinating with the South Royalton Fire and Rescue Squad, the South Royalton School, local churches, Vermont Law School, and community groups to respond to private homeowner relief and farmers who have lost crops and to sustain institutional damage.

As of Tuesday, Buxton estimates at least 60 volunteers have been dispatched to the food center at the Red Door Church and resident homes on Route 14 and North Windsor Street.

Volunteers are removing mud and water, helping to pack belongings, discarding contaminated fixtures, cleaning and other various tasks. There are also volunteers working at the food site, which is open to all, at the Red Door Church.

In houses, some of the work involves removing carpet and knocking down walls that are damaged beyond repair and pumping out cellars. In the school, besides cleaning, volunteers have needed to sort through contaminated books, files of sheet music, and discard contaminated musical instruments.

As individuals in need of assistance are identified, Buxton coordinates the need for help with the volunteers. The effort began by word of mouth when she notified some Vermont Law School students. She also posted the need for volunteers on her Facebook page. Buxton reports that Operation Revive Royalton came together in just a matter of hours.

With no funding available for Operation Revive Royalton, Buxton has drained her campaign account to buy the basic supplies needed to begin the clean-up.

Tunbridge Fire Chief John Durkee and Vermont Representative Sarah Buxton discuss coordination of volunteer help at the South Royalton School on Friday, September 2.

> *With no funding available for the Operation Revive Royalton, Buxton has drained her campaign.*

ROYALTON

Shumlin, FEMA Visit Royalton, *September 8*

Stuart Levasseur

Governor Peter Shumlin visited storm-ravaged South Royalton on Sunday, September 4, with other state and federal officials.

Speaking before the crowd gathered at the South Royalton Fire Station, Shumlin thanked the President for his fast response in declaring Vermont a disaster area, in the wake of Tropical Storm Irene.

Deputy Administrator Richard Serino from FEMA said he was impressed by the can-do spirit he found in Vermont. He found, he noted, people of all ages shoveling muck and working with dust masks and gloves in the clean-up effort.

Shumlin also announced that the environmental ban on removing gravel from the rivers and streams will be suspended, allowing towns to recover the gravel that has been washed into the rivers. This announcement received a huge crowd response from the otherwise somber audience.

Shumlin noted that in spite of the property damage, only four or fives lives were lost to the flood, (one is still unaccounted for). He urged caution in navigating the fragile roads.

The governor later went to the Perley farm in North Royalton, where he held a press conference in front of the gutted farmhouse.

The delegation toured the cow barn and talked with the farm manager Penny Severence, and her son Buddy. The Severences lost 25 cows, nearly half their herd. Several vehicles and equipment all were inundated with water.

Work crews have been busy for days, shoveling the river silt from the first floor and basement of the farmhouse. The entire contents of the house have been piled up in the yard; nothing can be salvaged.

"We're not going to rest until this farm and every piece of Vermont is put back better than Irene found it," Shumlin said.

> *The Severences lost 25 cows, nearly half their herd.*

Farm Report, *September 8*

Josey Hastings

Many vegetable farmers have experienced significant losses. Geo Honigford, owner of Hurricane Flats in South Royalton, lost all the produce in his fields, which are located on the banks of the White River.

"We're going to suffer from this," commented Honigford's wife, Sharon O'Connor, "but we still have a home. We didn't lose any animals or equipment."

Honigford himself could not be reached for comment via phone, as he was next door helping his neighbors whose houses were destroyed in the flood.

Governor Peter Shumlin, hugs South Royalton resident Aka Tatro, who lost her home to flood waters last Sunday. Tatro has registered for assistance from FEMA and said she will rebuild. Shumlin visited with residents and volunteers at the South Royalton Fire Department Sunday afternoon, thanking people for helping their neighbors after hurricane Irene.

Law School Takes Major Steps To Assist In Flood Emergency, *September 8*

SOUTH ROYALTON

Vermont Law School students, faculty and staff have been volunteering to help Vermont residents affected by Tropical Storm Irene, including offering legal aid and assistance filling out FEMA applications.

"Vermont Law School is determined to do whatever it can to help in our local community and across the region," said VLS Dean Jeff Shields.

Since the storm struck Sunday, hundreds of VLS students, faculty and staff have helped to clean up homes damaged by floodwaters in South Royalton and other communities. The students also are delivering food, beds and other supplies. Two students have suffered minor injuries during the clean-up.

FEMA Help

VLS's Land Use Clinic and South Royalton Legal Clinic will help residents to fill out FEMA applications in the VLS Library every day, through September 30.

The South Royalton Legal Clinic also will provide civil legal assistance.

If residents need additional legal advice, VLS volunteers will put them in contact with someone who can assist.

Personnel Assigned

VLS has assigned two of its staff—State Representative Sarah Buxton and Peg Trombly, a former chair of the South Royalton Selectboard—to work full time on relief efforts in local communities for the foreseeable future.

Another staff member, Abby Armstrong, a long-time volunteer in her hometown of Sharon, has been assigned to aid Sharon town officials this weekend.

The VLS faculty has loosened class attendance requirements, so students can continue to volunteer during normal class time and make up assignments later. VLS is allowing additional staffers to volunteer for short-term community relief efforts while continuing to receive their school paychecks.

Eight faculty and staffers whose homes are cut off have been put on paid administrative leave. Faculty and staffers whose commutes have been extended to several hours because of road closures are being allowed to work flexible schedules. VLS is also offering counseling to VLS students, staff, faculty and their relatives who need support.

The law school is soliciting cash donations for the town-wide Operation Revive Royalton to aid South Royalton and Royalton residents affected by Irene.

Big Weekend Still On

Alumni and Reunion Weekend on Sept. 16-18 will continue as scheduled, but with opportunities for alumni to volunteer for Irene relief efforts. VLS's classes started last week Wednesday, two days late, because of an electricity, telephone and Internet outage. All systems have been restored. The school itself did not escape substantial damage. Floodwaters caused an estimated $500,000 in damage on campus to two buildings, three riverside parking lots, the outdoor classroom and Internet server.

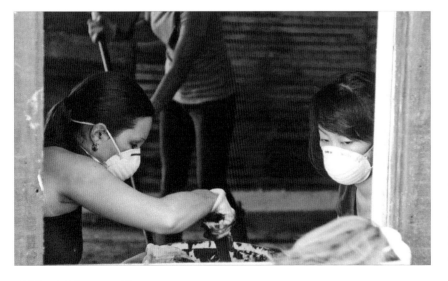

Volunteers help clean out mud and debris from the home of David Leighton on River Road in South Royalton. Here, second-year Vermont Law students Jennie Demjanick and Sara Li remove waterlogged sheetrock from inside the house.

Drew Alinovich's home on Route 14 in South Royalton was ravaged by flood damage, but he had an ace up his sleeve. As owner of Red Dog Restoration, Alinovich was able to round up his work crew to clean and gut the house, leaving it ready for restoration on Friday, September 2. After a long day's work, the crew erected a sign reading "Irene you hit like a Girl!" From left to right are T. Churchill, George Farrell, Cliff Lokey, Ryan Delaney, Wally Radicioni, Art Seymour, Drew Alinovich, Chris Kennison, Ethan Mozeika, and Ian Oxton.

Joanne James and Falko Schilling shovel mud from the basement of David Leighton's home in South Royalton on Friday, September 2.

J.P. Isabelle of Barre empties out a bucket of mud as volunteers help clean out debris from David Leighton's home.

First Branch

VERSHIRE

STRAFFORD

Vershire Restores Roads Taken Out by Irene

September 1

Laura Craft

Our town does not lie along a major waterway, although those living along the Ompompanoosuc, which parallels Route 113, might not agree.

Steve and Lorna Garrow's house is now much closer to the rearranged streambed. Luckily for them, the water filling up their garage and lapping at the door to their home rushed out when a second door in the garage was opened. Their horse spent Sunday afternoon and evening across the road on higher ground, but was happy to be back in her own stall on Monday, rolling around in the shavings as soon as she entered.

Several roads in town contain sections that were washed out completely, including Eagle Hollow, North Road and Eastman Crossroad.

Luckily, our town is rich with residents who have the equipment necessary to help make these roads passable, and by early Monday morning they were hard at work with excavators and dump trucks, assisting the road crew.

Route 113 was also closed for a time due to trees that had fallen across the road, and worries that the road surface had been undermined in places.

A neighbor whose basement was filling up made it to Bradford via Goose Green Road, and was lucky enough to find a sump pump for sale during the deluge.

One part of town maintained power during the entire storm, though further east toward West Fairlee, folks were without power for nearly 24 hours.

When I made a quick run to Baker's Store in Post Mills early Sunday morning, their power was already out. The Rivendell Schools, which were closed on Monday along with most schools in the state, were open once again on Tuesday.

Vershire, *September 8*

Laura Craft

We're now into our second week since Irene moved through, and the clean-up continues.

A group of Vershire folks, organized by Dawn Hancy, prepared and delivered food to a community dinner in Sharon this past Monday. Our town oven was used to bake 14 loaves of bread and roast three dozen ears of corn that were donated to the cause. The flood victims and volunteers in Sharon were very appreciative of the food and the support from a neighboring town.

Strafford Recovers from Flood: Route 103 Still Closed, *September 8*

John Frietag

While the aftermath of Irene remains a priority, there are signs that life in Strafford is returning to normal.

The only road remaining closed is Route 132 between South Strafford and Thetford. Due to the massive washout of the road, it will be quite a while before it is reopened.

In the meantime, the Strafford Selectboard and Road Foreman Jon MacKinnon continue to coordinate not only our own road crew, but many local contractors now engaged in repairing storm damages.

People continue to express appreciation for the long hours put in by many in handling this crisis.

A special thank-you dinner in appreciation for all who have helped out is planned for September 23 at Barrett Hall.

John Freitag works to remove nails from wood that used to make up the flood-damaged altar of Our Lady of Light Church in Strafford.

PART IV: Aftermath

Keith Hopkins of Pittsfield holding a flag found in the river during a clean-up day.

Paying for Irene, *October 27 Editorial*

M. D. Drysdale

Irene happened to all of us.

The storm happened to some of us worse than to others, of course, but it was a disaster for the whole state, one of the worst natural disasters in our history. And that's important to keep in mind as we face the prospect of paying for that disaster.

It won't be easy. The public infrastructure cost is loosely estimated at $1 billion in damage, mostly to state and local highways and bridges. That works out to more than $1500 for every man, woman, and child in Vermont.

Vermont's representative and senators in Congress are, appropriately, doing their best to see that existing federal emergency programs are directed to Vermont and are funded as generously as possible.

Certainly, the federal government's historic commitment to disaster relief gives it an important role. But realistically, those funds are limited. This year alone, as Representative Peter Welch pointed out in his letter to House Appropriations Committee leaders, 47 states experienced federally-declared disasters.

Gov. Peter Shumlin, too, when the topic of paying for Irene comes up, has mostly stuck with stressing the importance of keeping up the pressure on the feds to come up with disaster relief, generally avoiding any discussion of taxes.

But Vermont is going to have to do its share. Even the task of asking for federal relief should be easier if it can be shown that Vermonters are shouldering a good part of the burden of rebuilding.

And that will mean higher taxes, at least for an interim period.

Predictably, progressives like Senator Anthony Pollina are already demanding that the extra money come from "the rich," and indeed, wealthy Vermonters should contribute substantially to the work that needs to be done. But Irene happened to all of us, and the whole state needs to kick in to pay for it.

We don't have a tax expert at The Herald, but it seems from here that if most of the money is needed to repair our roads and bridges, substantial reimbursement should come from the users of those roads. That would mean a temporary increase in the gas tax.

Vermont's gas tax is now 24.9 cents per gallon, which should raise almost $88 million in 2013. Adding an extra 20 cents to the tax for two years could thus be expected to raise close to $140 million. Doubling the current tax would raise about $170 million in two years.

This would not be a popular option, and the gas tax is not particularly progressive, but it is focused exactly on the problem at hand, and it spreads the burden widely, including to out-of-staters who use our roads. And at a time when gas prices wobble up and down by 30 or 40 cents, an extra 20-cent tax would represent barely 5% more than we're paying now for gas.

Yes, an increase in the gas tax should be accompanied by a temporary rise in income taxes that would include the higher income brackets, and most individuals in those brackets would be understanding, we think, of the need to pitch in at a time of disaster. There are undoubtedly other ways to raise the needed money, though we think an increased sales tax, even temporary, should be off the table.

But pay for Irene we must, and because Irene happened to all of us, we all need to be part of the solution.

The gas tax is not particularly progressive, but it is focused exactly at the problem at hand.

White River:

Upper Branch

Hancock Selectboard Gets Report On Road Repairs, *October 13*

Commissioner James Leno stated at a selectboard meeting that Tunnel Brook and Killooleet Roads "are ready. They have been covered with crushed stone and rolled. Champlain Construction will be up on Blair Hill and will be trying to straighten out the corner and filling in the washouts. Then they will be rolled."

"Texas Falls is done, as far as it can be this year," Leno continued. "No paving will be completed until next spring. At that time, the work will go out to bid, with three bids needed. The latest update from Patrick Ross about the gravel bar issue up on Texas Falls is that the town has been given permission to remove and/or replace it and the riprap, although nothing has been finalized.

"Fasset Hill has gone out to bid, and three contractors from Middlebury have looked at it," Leno said. "The only road that has been emergency fixed, but not addressed, is Bettis Road. That will need to go out to bid."

Champlain Construction (Middlebury) will start working on Tucker Brook this week or early next week. They are also working on Taylor Brook Road, which sustained very little damage, and Leno said that "Shampeny Hill Road is also very drivable."

Leno said the town has replaced one culvert up on Buttles Road, and the Churchville Bridge is under contract from Phillips Engineering, with plans to start work by the first or second week of November. Once the work starts, the bridge will be closed, and there will be a temporary footbridge installed and in place for approximately two weeks. The estimated cost for the bridge is between $250,000 and $300,000.

"The only one that hasn't been done yet is Churchville," Leno said.

Leno assured everyone that Hancock would not be responsible for the proposed class 4 road that runs through Granville and Rochester, saying "This class 4 road is just a stop-gap to get everyone through the winter on Churchville."

Leno said that the town had hired Phillips Engineering for the design and planning stages of putting the road back together. The company has agreed to do the Churchville Bridge before the snow under the condition that the construction of the upper half be delayed until later spring or early summer.

Rochester, Hancock, & Granville Work Together on Road, *October 20*

Selectboard members from Granville, Hancock, and Rochester met Thursday, Oct. 13 in Granville to discuss a temporary emergency detour through TH #21.

The detour will allow residents of Churchville Road in Hancock a way out of their neighborhood this winter, since flooding destroyed the lower portion of their road during Hurricane Irene. Several people attending from Rochester and Hancock expressed their concerns that they will not be able to get out and emergency services, fuel trucks, power company and telephone company personnel will not be able to get to them if needed.

"We assured them that Granville would make sure that they would be able to get out and that emergency services and the utilities would be able to get to them as well," said Cheryl Sargeant of the Granville selectboard.

Rochester Selectboard Applies for Line of Credit To Make Repairs, *September 29*

Martha Slater

At the Rochester selectboard's Monday, Sept. 26 meeting, Andy Putnam of Riverbrook Farm asked the board about the Riverbrook Bridge, which was heavily damaged in the flooding from Hurricane Irene.

Board chair Larry Straus said it was still his intention to get a temporary bridge for that location, and that would be a FEMA reimbursable expense. He said he hoped it would happen before winter, but couldn't guarantee that. The riverbank there is somewhat compromised and an 80-90-foot span is needed.

Walt Pruiksma of the Tri-Town Snow Travelers spoke with the board about storm damage to class 4 roads and legal trails, which are used as recreational trails during the winter. He said he had hiked around and found that a number of trails in town are in "pretty bad shape." Pruiksma and Straus discussed damage in several specific areas, including Mount Cushman and Hooper Hollow. The board voted to give permission to the snowmobile club to work in the town right-of-way on the VAST trails.

Road foreman Dan Gendron prefaced his report on road repairs by noting, "We're gaining!" He spoke with the board about the rock crusher that the road crew has rented, which he said was working out well. On Saturday, the crew put out about 1200 yards of crushed rock on Brook Street and Liberty Hill.

Marvin Harvey noted that he'd had calls from residents on Buttles Road near the Hancock/Rochester town line, who now have to drive on Fiske Road to get to town, since their own road (which is in the town of Hancock) sustained so much damage. The board discussed work done on Fiske Road.

Water-sewer operator Terry Severy shared the good news that all the sewer flow was going where it was supposed to now.

ROCHESTER

Road foreman Dan Gendron prefaced his report on road repairs by noting, "We're gaining!"

Just shy of six weeks after Irene, a temporary bridge came in on six trucks over Brandon Gap to connect Routes 73 and 100.

Silt coats the fields around Rochester school.

Flood Aftermath Main Topic at Rochester School Board, *October 6*

The following summary of the Rochester School Board's September 20 meeting was written from minutes supplied to The Herald.

Board member Greg White congratulated Principal Mary Sue Crowley and the whole school staff for their "outstanding performance in the wake of Hurricane Irene." Crowley commended maintenance supervisor Tim Dunham on his "amazing job" working on flood damage to the school, meeting with an adjuster, completing a thorough "walk through," and receiving bids for renovations from Naylor and Breen and Travis Trombley of PC Construction.

The auditorium was affected by flood, especially the ceiling tiles, the hardwood floor and 188 seats. Some tiles contain asbestos—their replacement will be covered by the insurance, as well as the new seats. The White River Valley Players, who have used the auditorium many times, can advise on what kind of flooring to use. They are also willing to organize a fundraiser to cover a purchase of the rest of the seats, which though not flooded, were affected by the moisture. The concrete floor needs to be repainted.

The art room was cleaned by professionals, but the mess left behind was still an issue. Supt. John Poljacik pointed out that they could have the adjuster come back to determine whether the cleaning company had done their job properly. The principal's report included a thorough analysis of all damage and insurance coverage.

The Little League food shack was deposited at a neighbor's yard and needs to be removed from there. Tim Landwehr, who is in charge of Little League, will be consulted on what action needs to be taken.

While removing ceiling tiles in the auditorium, a few other areas (prop room, pipe elbows, light booth) covered in asbestos were discovered and should be removed at the same time at the school's expense if not covered by insurance.

Rochester Cemetery Commission Deals With The Unthinkable, *October 20*

Erosion prevention tarps at the damaged Woodlawn Cemetery

Martha Slater

During Hurricane Irene, flooding caused by Mason Brook disrupted at least 50 grave sites in a section of the Woodlawn Cemetery in Rochester. Although numerous vaults and caskets remained intact, some were broken, with bodies and bones dislodged.

For Rochester Cemetery Commission members, who normally handle maintenance issues, selling plots, and helping arrange burials, it's been almost eight weeks of dealing with the unthinkable. Woodlawn Cemetery is on a hill well above the White River and Mason Brook is so tiny that many people said afterwards that they never even knew there was a brook in the cemetery. Previous disastrous flooding in Vermont in 1927 and 1938 caused no damage to the cemetery.

Commission members Sue Flewelling, Marvin Harvey, chairman Tom Paquette, and Java Hubbard met last Thursday with the Herald to share updated information about the recovery and restoration process. The other member of the committee, Lisa Steventon, was unable to attend.

Immediately after the flood, Sunday, August 28, commission members could not contact each other, since electricity and phones were out. Two of them, Paquette and Flewelling, live

> **Previous disastrous flooding in Vermont in 1927 and 1938 caused no damage to the cemetery.**

on Route 73, which was cut off from the rest of town when the bridge from Route 100 collapsed into the White River.

"It was Tuesday afternoon before we could get together and meet with Tom Harty of Day's Funeral Home, who had managed to get over Bethel Mountain by ATV to help out," Flewelling said. "Prior to that, several volunteers had covered and secured some remains that were in the immediate vicinity."

During the following week, more volunteers came to help—local residents, as well as people from as far away as South Carolina. Flewelling spent three weeks sitting vigil in the cemetery driveway in her lawn chair for many hours each day—answering questions of family members, offering reassurance, collecting information, and keeping out the overly curious. She also received between 400-500 calls from relatives wanting information.

Lots of Help

"The commission has had a huge amount of help from volunteers and professionals from all over," she said. "People like the state medical examiner, Tom Harty, security officers who came from UVM and Middlebury and Montpelier and the state police, and many more, did so much to help us."

Searching took place as far south as the Liberty Hill Bridge, using a foot search, dog team search, and water search on float boards. People need to be aware that if we have more flooding, as debris from flooding is cleaned up, and the landscape changes over time, they will quite possibly find remains downstream.

The bodies of 24 individuals and numerous bones were recovered. They were placed in new metal caskets and sealed in new vaults with the help of the Vermont Funeral Directors Association, and the bodies, caskets, and the exterior of each vault were marked with an identification number.

The vaults will remain at the cemetery until re-interment, which will be arranged by the cemetery commission, and Day Funeral Home, after input from the families. Bones set adrift during flooding will be re-interred together in a single container. The office of the Chief Medical Examiner in Burlington is providing temporary storage of bones.

Commission members noted that some remains that were found have yet to be identified, so they would welcome information from family members who think a relative's grave may have been among those disrupted.

"This process of identifying remains is an ongoing thing," Hubbard noted. "Samples have been taken by the medical examiner's office and will be kept up to five years."

Bruce and Patrice (Lary) Buxton of Rochester were among those who had family members' graves disrupted as a result of the flooding. It was a traumatic experience for them, but they had great praise for the help they got from the cemetery commission.

"We were really comforted by their thoughtfulness, efficiency, and thoroughness," Bruce Buxton commented. "They really had all their bases covered."

Cemetery's Future

"People ask us what we're going to do with the cemetery," Paquette said. "The ideal situation would be to rebuild the section of the cemetery that washed out and re-inter the remains of those who were there. That's our aim."

All of this will cost money that isn't in the commission's modest annual budget of $14,000. It's been estimated that the total cost of repairs, including the large amounts of fill needed to rebuild the area that was washed away, could be close to $1 million. The cost may possibly be partially covered by FEMA, but that's by no means certain, Flewelling stressed.

Woodlawn Cemetery is now open, and the remains there are secure, but signs warn folks to "enter at your own risk."

It's been estimated that the total cost of repairs, including the large amounts of fill needed to rebuild the area that was washed away, could be close to $1 million.

National Guard members from New Hampshire delivered a large tent to cover exposed caskets left by the hurricane.

Angelique Lee and Jason Hayden worked with the White River Partnership to coordinate a Tweed River Clean Up on Sunday, October 16. Twenty-five volunteers showed up that morning. WRP Board member Geo Honigford of Royalton helped on site. "We were able to walk most of the flood plains and river banks (the water was very high due to recent rain) from The Clear River Tavern north to Guernsey Brook," Lee reported. "It was a very successful day for debris removal, but there is still more work to be done. Once snowmobile bridges are rebuilt, we will have access to the east side of the river." Here, Kiernan Lackney of Rutland loads a TV satellite dish onto the trash pile.

Tweed River

Pittsfield

Stockbridge Road Goal: 'Everyone on a Plowable Road by Winter,' *October 6*

Vance Stratton helps guide Cid Hotchkiss's bulldozer on River Road in Stockbridge.

Martha Slater

Just over four weeks after the flooding caused by Hurricane Irene, Mark Doughty and Mark Pelletier of the Stockbridge selectboard, Road Commissioner David Brown, and Senate President Pro-Tem John Campbell, took Governor Shumlin to the site of the Peavine Restaurant to show him the gravel deposited there.

"We asked him if they could have access to that and he said he'd try to make that happen."

"Last Tuesday when we took the governor around, one of the things we wanted to talk about with him was the 18 homes in Chalet Village on Route 100 that were damaged," Doughty explained. "The homes never flooded until the town was prohibited from taking gravel out of the Tweed River, so when that happened, the silt built up and forced the river to move over. Now, when that river floods, it goes right into Chalet Village.

"We've asked for permission to move the river back against South Hill. If they won't let us do that, those folks there are out of luck because it will continue to flood.

"We've been told that there might be hazard mitigation money for those individuals who want the town to acquire that property, but we don't know what the chances of that are right now. We wanted to show him that and get him thinking about what our options might be."

"Most of our roads took significant hits," Doughty added, "and we only have three pickup trucks, a grader and backhoe for town equipment, so if it wasn't for the help from outside contractors, it would take us years to get our roads back in shape.

"Fortunately for us, a lot of people in town have heavy equipment, and right after the flood, those folks jumped into their equipment and started working on their roads and worked their way out to meet others who were doing the same thing." River Road is now open to Bethel, "and that's the suggested route in and out of town, because Route 107 is expected to be closed until at least Thanksgiving. Dartt Hill is open to Camp Brook Road and that's another east-west route. It's our plan to have everyone in town on a plowable road by winter."

> *"Now, when that river floods, it goes right into Chalet Village."*
> *Mark Doughty*

STOCKBRIDGE

Havoc in the Hills: Rain, Ruin, and Rescue, Part II

Members of an evacuation team of Sheriff's Office and state Fish & Wildlife personnel, plus several unpaid volunteers, pause to rest during an hour-long journey on washed-out ATV trails to transport two residents of Davis Hill Road in Stockbridge to Bethel.

Relief, Red Tape, and Revival, *September 29*

Tom Hill

At high noon on Thursday, Sept. 2, four days after Hurricane Irene turned my life upside down, the caravan arrived.

Half a dozen mud-caked all-terrain vehicles crawled out of the woods into my neighbor's yard, carrying a nine-man crew: a Fish and Wildlife officer, a couple of deputy sheriffs, and several unpaid volunteers.

The day before, I had been semi-evacuated up the ravaged ruin of Davis Hill Road in Stockbridge from my home, to await final rescue from my uninhabitable abode.

These rugged guys were about to take my neighbor (call him Bob) and me, plus our two dogs and a small portion of our worldly goods stuffed into backpacks and duffel bags, down the mountain over a network of old trails. None of them were on any current map. None had been maintained for generations.

Flatlanders may require illumination about the word "road." If you think a road is anything that can be traversed in a Chrysler moving at the posted speed limit—well, that's not what a road is in Vermont.

Here's the rule of thumb: If no trees are growing in it that can't be flattened by a half-ton vehicle moving at 20 miles per hour, it's a road.

The load-out was quick and efficient: goods stashed in small, open-air cargo bays (covered with tarps to protect them from the mud we would pass through); Bob and his dog in a large, red Toyota rig ahead of me; myself in the passenger seat of an olive-colored Polaris; my toy poodle Buddy Mac clutched in my arms.

We were off into the trees.

No way, I thought several times, trying to communicate telepathically with the deputy who held my life and his

*If not for ATVs,
I might still be
up there.*

steering wheel in the same hands. Don't try this! You can't get up a slope that steep! You can't crawl over a rock that big! You can't ford a stream that wide! There's no way you can — please don't even — you wouldn't — you couldn't —

He would. He could. He did.

We paused about 30 minutes into our journey so the caravan's point man, Fish & Wildlife officer Keith Gallant, could check in with headquarters by radio. Buddy Mac was a trembling ball of fuzzy Jell-O in my lap.

I have not always been a fan of ATVs. My stereotype was a dark one: drunken yahoos tearing up fragile trails, terrorizing wildlife, etc. I knew they could be useful in law enforcement, emergency response, and getting around in the farther places, but that part was pretty abstract.

Well, an hour after our evacuation had begun—after we had lurched, slewed, pitched and yawed through realms no motor vehicle should have been able to negotiate, once I stood again on solid ground in the land of hot showers and remote controls—I saw things differently.

If not for ATVs, I might still be up there.

Chains of Command

After any natural disaster comes lack of clarity about chains of command. However dedicated and competent, each responder has a different take on what should be done; what will be done; who will do it; how much of what needs to be done already has been done; and how long it will take to do what hasn't been done yet.

When numerous entities—from the town constable through the county sheriff's office to the Federal Emergency Management Agency and the National Guard—work across a wide spectrum of resources, experience, local savvy and protocol, one man's hammer is another man's nail.

Which brings us back to Keith Gallant, reporting into his hand-held squawk box that we were about halfway out. What, he asked, was he supposed to do with us then?

He listened, then asked Bob and me where we wanted to go. We supposed that Stockbridge Common was as good a place as any to ponder our options. This he reported to headquarters.

And off we lurched, slewed, pitched and yawed.

*You can't get up a
slope that steep!
You can't crawl
over a rock that
big! You can't
ford a stream
that wide!*

Brought out somewhere off of North Road in Barnard onto the first pavement we had seen in several days, Bob and I (and our animals) were handed off to two Motor Vehicle Department officers, who piled us and our belongings into a pickup truck.

Off we went. But not toward Stockbridge. We were heading north.

"Where are we going?" I asked.

Bethel, the driver replied.

"We're trying to get to Stockbridge," I said.

"Nobody told me anything about Stockbridge," he answered. "We were told to take you to Bethel."

And, tethered to the frail reed of his instructions, Bethel it was.

First Stop

Specifically, Whitcomb High School, which had been set up as a temporary shelter. Two disheveled human beings and two freaked-out canines were off-loaded into the parking lot.

Where we were told we couldn't stay, because we had dogs.

Our misery was now industrial-strength. But local liberal activist Ola O'Dell was present, and witnessed our plight. Announcing that we could spend that night at her home nearby, she took us there in her car, which bore bumper stickers championing many a left-of-center cause.

Her old-fashioned home radiated the charming, slightly rumpled gentility of a busy life, passionately lived. Also in residence was a mild-mannered canine of hunting-dog stock. Big as a boxcar. Bob's similarly laid-back pet weighed slightly less than a Clydesdale.

The rooms in this house were mostly not very large. As these two restless behemoths constantly repositioned themselves, the overall effect suggested a demolition derby between two battleships in a phone booth.

Being about the size of a pound cake, Buddy Mac took issue with this shifting geometry, especially since the two gentle giants wanted to know more about him. Normally sociable, if high-strung, Buddy Mac doesn't visit the outer world much. After that roller-coaster gallivant through the woods, his sense of personal space was in tatters.

So, he responded to those furry, inquisitive Zeppelin heads by snapping at them. He wasn't really trying to bite anybody. He was saying, "I've had a long day, Mount Rushmore. Get out of my FACE!"

As passably peaceable as was the night that followed, the nerves of all concerned called for another arrangement.

Long story short: I landed in a spartan room in a dormitory at Vermont Technical College in Randolph Center, which was being operated as a shelter. Coordinated by Dave Sanville, Gifford Medical Center's chief financial officer and pastor at the Assembly of God Church in Bethel, a consortium of volunteers was seeing to the needs of several displaced people who had nowhere else to stay.

Pets weren't allowed (fights, fleas, barking, howling at the moon, etc.), so Buddy Mac checked in at the Country Animal Hospital in Bethel. Here he would stay, without charge, for most of nearly three weeks as I sought a dog-permitting alternative. His abandonment issues had gone ballistic.

Stop and Review

A review of my situation at that point:

One-lane bridge linking rented home to Davis Hill Road: gone. Davis Hill Road, leading down to Stony Brook Road: gone. Stony Brook Road, leading out to state Route 107: substantially gone. State Route 107, leading to the rest of the world: washed out for miles in both directions.

My car: marooned through the winter at my home. Access: an eight-mile hike over boulders, chasms, and fallen trees.

Winter: coming fast. Timetable for repair of Davis Hill, Stony Brook, and Route 107: as soon as enough gravel to fill the Grand Canyon could be trucked in—if the landslides would stop long enough for exhausted crews to get the job done.

Me: working a part-time job at Whitcomb High School, trying to rebuild myself professionally (with unspectacular results) after an unsuccessful foray into free-lance writing. Need for car, clothing and home (typical cost: one month's rent, plus two months' rent up front as a deposit): immediate, absolute and desperate.

Alice in Wonderland

Thus began my foray into the Alice-in-Wonderland netherworld of federal bureaucracy. Red tape. Paperwork. Hours spent online, on the phone, on hold, telling my story again and again and again.

What one's options were, and with whom one should discuss them, varied greatly, depending on whom one contacted. Players included FEMA, the Red Cross, the Small Business Administration, and—at a lower level of nuance and complication—the Community Action center, the local food shelf and clothing drive, etc.

Bethel's town hall served as one of many clothing drops in the area, and donors were generous. When Gov. Peter Shumlin attended a "people's meeting" there on Sept. 4, he was almost comically dwarfed by the heaps of shirts, sweaters, dresses, pants, sheets and towels that surrounded him.

The shirt and socks I'm wearing now? Bethel Town Hall.

As for the private sector, I called the company that insures my automobile and explained the situation, hoping they'd pay for a rental car.

Is your car damaged?

No. It's eight miles up beyond the end of the world, but it's undamaged.

Is it drivable?

Yes. I can drive it fifty feet before plunging into a ravine, where it will remain until the next ice age buries it under a glacier.

I'm sorry, sir. If the car is undamaged, you're not covered.

Had I wrecked the car trying to get off the mountain, they'd help me. Since I'd had the good sense not to try, I was on my own. So I rented a car, which cost more money than I earn. As we granola crunchers say, this was unsustainable.

I applied for a FEMA grant to replace the bridge at my rented driveway, which is owned by economic exiles in Kentucky. I

An excavator at work in the White River along washed-out Route 107 in Stockbridge.

> *Thus began my foray into the Alice-in-Wonderland netherworld of federal bureaucracy.*

learned that if you live there, but don't own it, FEMA won't help you. If you own it, but don't live there, FEMA won't help you.

Over-the-phone FEMA folks were mostly polite, even sympathetic. But they were merely the outermost tendrils of the beast; they had no control over the rules by which the beast behaves.

As for the Small Business Administration, which does about 90 percent of its business in the form of loans to hard-hit individuals, I wasn't eligible for SBA assistance, either. I don't make enough money.

If my income were higher, I could get money? Yes.

Facebook to the Rescue

Much has been written in this publication recently about the generosity and heroism that poured forth in communities affected by Irene. My experience at the receiving end of this juggernaut of compassion was breath-taking and life-affirming.

It's trite, but true: If you want to witness the overall decency of nearly everybody, drop a disaster on them and watch what happens.

Take Facebook. Prior to Irene, I never had much use for Facebook. I had put up a Facebook page, though I wasn't quite sure why. I didn't spend much time nurturing it. Everybody Was Doing It; so there.

But it was via Facebook that much of the response to Irene took form. Pages dedicated to helping the storm's victims sprang up immediately. Some postings asked for help; others offered it. Want to know when the next public meeting is in Rochester? Check Facebook. Need a crew to muck out a basement in Pittsfield? Post it on Facebook. Got a wheelbarrow to loan? Post it on Facebook.

Government websites might be several days behind the curve. When a remote road in Gilead was fixed, the news would be on Facebook within minutes.

Connections were sometimes so indirect, via multiple degrees of separation, that it wasn't always clear how assistance happened, or who had talked to whom to make it so. Within a few days of my Facebook post about lacking a car, total strangers in Plainfield had called me to offer the loan of a car through December.

That car is out in the driveway now.

Whose driveway? Ah: the Randolph Center driveway of John and Carol Doss. Facebook wasn't the only grapevine in town. Members of this church chatted with members of that church, who spoke to somebody, who knew someone, who had heard that a refugee from Davis Hill was staying at the Vermont Tech shelter and needed a place to stay with his dog.

So I got a call from John Doss, who offered me and Buddy Mac a comfortable bedroom and house-roaming privileges while we put our lives back together.

Buddy Mac loves it here. There's a big back porch that he patrols vigilantly, barking canine expletives at every chipmunk he sees.

Safe, sweet home—for now.

So here comes the future, as usual. Where will I live a year from now? What will I be doing? Not a clue. Whatever I may have achieved by then, I am unlikely to have done it by myself. The hands of friends, the hands of strangers, will steady the scaffolding, whether I notice it or not.

Buddy Mac will claim too much credit for what goes right. As usual.

He won't be doing it by himself, either. Nobody does.

(Tom Hill is, among other things, a writer and musician temporarily housed in Randolph Center.)

Roxbury Fish Hatchery, *October 27*

Sandy Vondrasek

The historic Roxbury Fish Hatchery on Route 12A took a big hit August 28. Floodwaters scoured the narrow valley, wiping out the hatchery's six outdoor ponds and flushing an estimated 65,000 brook and rainbow trout downstream to doubtful fates. Thousands of brook trout eggs in incubators in a basement "hatch house" were lost, as well, due to contamination by floodwaters.

A springhouse at the north end of the seven-acre lot was ripped away, the hatchery's driveways turned into gullies, and its three quaint, clapboarded buildings took in varying amounts of floodwater and silt.

Two months later, although the 1891 hatchery still shows evidence of Irene's wrath, its staff of three is already "pushing on with production," said Supervisor Jeremy Whalen on Tuesday. He and the hatchery's two "fish culturists" are daily tending 120,000 recently-hatched trout fry in the basement of the main building, for stocking in 2013 and 2014.

But there won't be any sizeable fish in the hatchery's outdoor ponds next spring for school kids to feed, and there will be fewer brook and rainbow trout stocked in Vermont waters next spring.

Whalen said this week that while the hatchery will certainly be restored, outside work is temporarily on pause, while state officials consider the smartest way to rebuild.

Whalen admits he'd be happy to see the hatchery's unique arrangement of gravity-flow ponds—all six of which were "blown out" on August 28—restored. Roxbury's exclusive reliance on the ponds—supplied with a combination of spring, brook, and sometimes well water—is unique among the state's six hatcheries. Concrete raceways with pumped water are more commonly used,

> *"There really isn't any difference between us and a dairy farm. Fish have to be cleaned and fed, pretty much every day."*
> *Jeremy Whalen*

Roxbury Hatchery Manager Jeremy Whalen shows how flooding from Tropical Storm Irene destroyed the facility's pond, releasing tens of thousands of trout.

Third Branch
ROXBURY

Whalen said, but they lead to some fin wear-and-tear on the fish, as they jockey and jostle in the raceways.

Nice Fish

Roxbury is known for turning out "really nice fish," he said.

Its open ponds provide a natural fluctuation of temperature, and the cold, mountain water is "perfect for brook trout," he said.

Roxbury's pond-raised trout also learn to "key in on insect hatches," whereas fish in raceways or covered ponds are exclusively fed on commercially-produced grain products.

One drawback of the system, however, is that it leaves the fish vulnerable to predators. Whalen estimates that the hatchery loses 15-20% of its stock to predation by mink, otter, heron, osprey, and raccoons each year. Roxbury is also unique in that it is the only hatchery raising fish for Vermont's trophy trout stocking program. Six thousand two-year-old brook trout, each 12-14 inches long, were among the 65,000 fish lost in the recent flooding.

Not all trout were flushed out, though. An estimated 10,000-15,000 yearling trout, each about seven inches long, remain trapped in the shallow remains of what was once a six-foot deep pond on the southern end of the narrow property.

If these survivors pass disease testing, Whalen said, they'll be placed in streams in the next couple of weeks.

Like many Vermonters, Whalen has a deep affection for the Roxbury Fish Station, with its funky, summer-camp charm. He remembers his parents bringing him there once or twice a summer when he was a kid, to feed the fish.

Whalen, now 34, worked for several years at Roxbury as one of the hatchery's two fish culturists. A 1999 graduate of the fish culture program at SUNY Cobleskill, he was recently promoted to supervisor, following the retirement of Ralph Barber. Today, Whalen supervises two fish culturists, Nate Olson and Sara Nebelecky, both recent college graduates in their mid-20s.

Historic Place

The Roxbury Fish Station is on the National Register of Historic Sites, and there are some arguments to be made for restoring it to its traditional form.

It would take up to $350,000 to restore the hatchery to its former condition, Whalen noted. State and FEMA officials are now confabbing on how to proceed, with an eye to minimizing flood damage in the future.

While state and FEMA officials debate how to proceed with the hatchery rebuild, Whalen and his two assistants are focused, for the most part, on the hands-on work of taking care of 120,000 trout fry, while plugging away at clean-up tasks.

With the trout fry now safely transferred from incubation racks to long tanks in the hatch room, the hatchery staff is getting ready to receive a shipment of 450,000 Atlantic salmon eggs. Whalen, Olson, and Nebelecky will watch over these as they hatch and mature into 3/4-inch fry that will be put in the White River Watershed in the late spring, in a cooperative arrangement with the federal salmon hatchery in Bethel.

"There really isn't any difference between us and a dairy farm," Whalen commented. "Fish have to be cleaned and fed, pretty much every day."

BRAINTREE

Sam Paddock's family has farmed on Riford Brook since 1958. He moved eight beef cattle to safety just before he lost the back twenty feet of his barn to flood waters.

Bill Tufts in front of his flood damaged garage on Thayer Brook Road.

Shirley and George Rogers have lived in their Braintree ranch on Rte 12A for three-and-a-half decades. In all that time they've had water in their basement only once. Irene flooded their entire home to a depth of almost three feet, ruining seven rooms of furniture, appliances and the furnace. While on the outside their home looks almost untouched, like many others they've had to gut the property, removing carpeting, linoleum, underlayment, sheet rock, insulation, electrical outlets, and all the lower kitchen cabinets.

Olney Will Bring Baseball Moguls To Randolph, *October 6*

By M. D. Drysdale

Both Theo Epstein, general manager of the Boston Red Sox, and Brian Cashman, GM of the New York Yankees, will take part in a baseball discussion in Randolph Nov. 12 to raise money for farm relief in Vermont.

Among the dozens of post-Irene fundraisers in and out of Vermont, only one of them is named "Going to Bat for Vermont Farmers." And only one of them—that one—will bring several of Major League Baseball's biggest names to Vermont Technical College.

A unique effort to help Vermont farmers damaged by Irene is being organized by Sam Lincoln and Buster Olney, brothers who grew up on a Randolph Center dairy farm. Lincoln has stayed in agriculture here, while Olney has become one of the nation's most prominent sports commentators—somebody with lots of friends in Major League Baseball who can be called upon to help.

And they have responded. Some of those friends will be present at Vermont Tech on November 12, and many others have donated items for an online baseball-related raffle.

Two who will actually be present are the general managers of the two teams with the most famous rivalry in baseball: Theo Epstein of the Boston Red Sox and Brian Cashman of the New York Yankees. Coming right after one of the most dramatic climaxes of a regular season, the appearance of both Epstein and Cashman talking baseball in the same room is expected to be a huge draw.

Epstein has been the Boston general manager for a decade, and in that time, the Red Sox have won two World Series. Cashman has been general manager of the Yankees for the last 14 seasons, and in that time, the Yankees have won four World Series.

Another general manager—Neal Huntington of the Pittsburgh Pirates, who grew up on a New Hampshire farm–will be present, as well. Then there's Buster Olney himself. He covered the Yanks for the New York Times for several years and is now a prominent ESPN columnist, sought out constantly for his views on baseball. He's also one of just 575 sportswriters who get to vote on Hall of Fame ballots.

Free Flood Relief Help on Main Street, *October 20*

A storefront of Randolph's Main Street is offering household items free of charge to anyone who lost items in the flooding and needs help getting their home back together.

George Rich owns the storefront. He is continuing to accept donations of kitchen items, including small appliances, as well as bedding, winter outerwear, toys, books, and small furniture at the storefront, which opened about a month ago.

An orange sign in the window states "flood relief."

Thrift Shop Hosts Giveaway of Clothing this Weekend, *October 27*

Prices at Gifford's Thrift Shop are always low (really low), but this weekend the Thrift Ship is going one step further—a giveaway of adult and children's clothing.

Due to the generosity of the public following Irene, the Thrift Shop has "excess amounts of clothing to pass on," according to manager Dianne Elias.

Thus, the Thrift Shop will have clothing under a tent this weekend, both Saturday and Sunday from 8 a.m.-4 p.m., while supplies last.

Cash donations will be accepted for the benefit of flood victims, but the clothing will be free.

> *The appearance of both Epstein and Cashman talking baseball in the same room is expected to be a huge draw.*

RANDOLPH

Bethel's Pleasant Street Hard-Hit by Irene
Nine Mobile Homes, Four Houses Damaged

September 29

Sandy Vondrasek

Bethel's River Street wasn't the only part of the town hard-hit by Tropical Storm Irene. Waters from the Third Branch invaded much of Pleasant Street (Route 12, north of Bethel village), badly damaging nine mobile homes in Richards Trailer Park, and four houses plus outbuildings on the east side of the road. The Bethel-U-Save grocery also lost its inventory to water damage and is currently closed.

The flooding was manageable, residents said, until a sudden "surge" pushed up water levels by two feet or more that afternoon.

Among those coping with close-to-uninhabitable conditions since the flood are Ted LaHaye and Ruth Gagain-Scali, who live in a mobile home on the north end of Richards Park.

LaHaye, 72, takes care of Gagain-Scali, 81, who has very limited mobility, due to medical issues. LaHaye said floodwaters starting rolling into the park that afternoon.

"Everybody on our side was evacuated except us," he recalled. "The firemen wanted us out, but I said, 'Whatever happens, happens.'"

Almost immediately after the firemen left, he added, "We got the surge."

"It hit us first. I opened up the back door and two feet of water flooded the whole place. I opened the front door up, and all the water started going out," he said.

"Two old people, stuck here through the whole thing," LaHaye commented ruefully.

Since then, LaHaye has been working daily, 7:30 a.m.-midnight, to clean and dry out their home: "I lost 15 pounds; I hope I keep it off."

After cleaning out the silt, he put

> *"It hit us first. I opened up the back door and two feet of water flooded the whole place."*

Grateful for each other, despite huge losses to the flood, Sally and Charlie Gilman have lived for years at the corner of Camp Brook Road and Route 12 in Bethel. "Water was up to the stoop in the last two floods," said Charlie, adding, "You'd think we'd have sold it." This time the water rose to four feet in the first floor.

BETHEL

Inside their mobile home, Ted LaHaye and Ruth Gagain-Scali have been sleeping in their chairs, the mattresses ruined in the flood. The floors are covered with cardboard to help soak up leftover moisture.

down layer after layer of newspapers and cardboard to absorb moisture from the floor, and ran fans to keep the air moving. Mold started to grow, anyway, and LaHaye has scraped and bleached the floors and walls, to keep it at bay.

Nighttimes, LaHaye sleeps in a rocking chair, with his feet propped up on a kitchen chair, and Gagain-Scali sleeps in her recliner.

More recently, he has spent time packing up their belongings, as it is clear that they can't spend the winter in their home.

Part of the trailer now has no electricity, and the two-year-old furnace and all the heating ducts are wrecked.

They are looking for a place to stay for the winter, and exploring whatever kind of help they can get from FEMA and other agencies, to buy a new trailer for the park.

"In a couple of weeks, I hope we can get where we are ready to go," LaHaye added. "Where we're gonna go—that's the scary part."

First Flood

Trailer park co-owner Tim Aldrighetti said his father built the 21-unit park in the 1950s. The land, he said, is in the 100-year flood plain; this is the first time it ever flooded.

The park, being "just the land," is not eligible for flood insurance, he said. And, although two feet of water surged in, there was not much damage to the land itself.

However, the entire front row of homes, including the Gagain-Scali/LaHaye trailer, were "pretty much destroyed," Aldrighetti said.

Clean-up has been intense for everybody.

Aldrighetti said he carted 42 loads of refuse in a tandem-axle dump trailer to the transfer station.

He may or may not get reimbursed for the $5000 disposal bill, but "it was the least I can do," he said.

Aldrighetti said that four of his tenants who lost homes have already bought new units to put back on their lots.

He is in the process of upgrading those lots, adding gravel, compacting it, and putting down a six-inch concrete pad for the units. He is not allowed to raise the lots, but residents can bring up

> *"By the time I got my horse out, the water was almost up to my waist," said Turgeon, who is Bethel's postmaster.*

Ted LaHaye, who lives with and cares for his friend Ruth Gagain-Scali in the mobile home park along Route 12 in Bethel, reckons that he has been working from seven until midnight everyday since the flood, trying to salvage what he can from the rubble. Gagain-Scali, who has severe health problems, worries that she will not be able to find a new home before winter.

the level of the units via cement blocks.

Aldrighetti is now working with FEMA to have the destroyed units removed and dismantled off site. Aldrighetti said FEMA initially wanted to have the units dismantled where they sat, but he pointed out that mold and other toxins would be released. With other residents still there and a school nearby, that would be a bad idea, he pointed out.

Aldrighetti said that the other 12 units in the park are okay, though several had some water damage.

Working with FEMA, he said, has been "frustrating and overwhelming" for all parties, especially residents whose lives were already in disarray.

"It's so involved," he added. "I keep learning; at last night's meeting I learned new things."

"We will be revitalized," Aldrighetti said of the trailer park. "We will have a pig roast on the anniversary of Irene for all the residents and all those flooded

out. We are trying to put this behind us."

The trailer park was covered with two feet of water; the homes across the street, he noted, got hit by four to five feet of flooding.

Deep Waters

Renee Turgeon, who lives in one of those Pleasant Street homes with her husband, Butch Carrier, this week recalled looking out her window on August 28 and seeing "a wall of water" rolling towards the house.

She headed out to get her horse from the barn behind the house.

"By the time I got my horse out, the water was almost up to my waist," said Turgeon, who is Bethel's postmaster.

She and her husband crossed the street to higher ground, "and stood there, in the dark, holding a horse."

Bethel Selectman Neal Fox, there assisting firefighters, told Turgeon to walk the horse up to his place, as he had an empty stall.

Since then, Turgeon and Carrier have

It's the end of a truly labor intensive Labor Day for Jon Hodgdon and volunteers Kep Taylor and Tyler Harwell. With help from many, Hodgdon has managed to clear several feet of mud from the basement of his Bethel business, Miller Machine.

Terri and Jon Hodgdon in their "mud boots" are hopeful as the Labor Day weekend draws to a close at Miller Machine Shop.

Stephen Wright, of Randolph, teaches glacial geology at the University of Vermont. Extreme flooding exposed important geological data. On August 30 he biked up the severely damaged Bethel Gilead Road to study sand and gravel pushed into Vermont from the far north during the last ice age.

been living in their camper—luckily it was still parked at Lake Champagne. They are among the lucky folks who have flood insurance. However, they have already spent $10,000 out-of-pocket, just on clean-up.

They are hopeful—after paying for flood insurance for the past five years—that the money will come through.

The basement, which had spilt fuel, needed a haz-mat pump, and EPA contractors have since come by to remove oil residues, she said.

Over the past weeks, the house has been completely cleaned and gutted and is now ready for the contractors to move in to do the extensive repairs needed in the home, and to pour a new foundation for the barn.

Turgeon, who has already lined up workers, had hoped to move back into their repaired home by the holidays.

"All that is holding this up is the dollars—I am hoping they are there," she said.

Toxic Salmon, *October 6*

Sandy Vondrasek

The multi-agency commission in charge of the Atlantic salmon restoration program voted last Thursday on mixed fates for the salmon that survived August 28 flooding at the White River National Fish Hatchery in Bethel.

Because floodwaters may have carried an invasive aquatic plant called didymo into the hatchery, the Connecticut River Atlantic Salmon Commission (CRASC) agreed that none of the 13,000 survivors should be placed in didymo-free waters.

According to Ken Sprankle, executive assistant for CRASC, several thousand small juvenile salmon that were inside the hatchery's main building during the flood will be released into the wild, but in waters where didymo is already present— the lower stem of the White River.

The balance of the remaining, older fish, some of them valuable brood stock, will be killed, cleaned, and made available to a number of Native American tribes in the northeast for ceremonial purposes, he said.

Still to be decided is the fate of the 450,000 lake trout that were being raised at the Bethel hatchery for release next spring in Lakes Erie and Ontario. Those lakes are didymo-free, and extra DNA testing is being done to gauge the extent of contamination in hatchery waters. A first round of testing showed no didymo, but a more sophisticated test has been ordered, Sprankle said.

Tropical Storm Irene's high volume

of water may have scoured out much of the White River's didymo population, he surmised. Didymo, first found in the watershed in 2007, forms dense, slimy mats on river rocks and effectively destroys fish habitat.

All fish at the Bethel hatchery have to be removed so it can be decontaminated and repaired. Flooding damaged some hatchery buildings, compromised the entire water system, and contaminated other equipment and infrastructure.

Future Role Cloudy

The White River National Fish Hatchery will be out of commission for at least one year, and possibly several, while repairs are done. The temporary closure will put a substantial dent in the Atlantic salmon program, as Bethel has been producing about 60% of the fry stocked in the Connecticut River basin, noted Sprankle, who is also the Connecticut River coordinator for the U.S. Fish and Wildlife Service.

Vermont's Roxbury Fish Hatchery will continue to raise Atlantic salmon fry, and a Connecticut state hatchery will continue to raise salmon smolts for release into the ocean. Sprankle estimated, however, that three million fry—instead of the usual six million—will be released into the Connecticut River watershed next spring. The U.S. Fish and Wildlife Service has not yet requested any federal funds for repairs at the Bethel hatchery, estimated to cost upwards of $8 million.

Aid Center Told To Vacate Town Hall,

September 29

M. D. Drysdale

The emergency aid center in the Bethel Town Hall was being dismantled yesterday afternoon (Wednesday), per the orders of the town selectboard.

Starting a few days after the August 28 flood, the newly-renovated town hall has been a flurry of activity. It was a drop-off spot for donated clothing and personal items, a center for postings matching needs and resources, and a nerve center for directing the energies of literally hundreds of volunteers.

The emergency effort was being coordinated by Amber Taft, who has worked 8-10 hours a day for three weeks, all unpaid. She's been helped by several lieutenants and dozens of volunteers.

The selectboard, however, has been uneasy about turning over its prized building to an open-ended emergency effort. They have noted that the emergency use would make paid rentals impossible.

At a meeting last week, the board ruled that the building should be cleared by this Monday, the 26th.

That didn't happen, as Bethel resident and State Senator Dick McCormack tried to negotiate a compromise that would allow the operations in the town hall to be consolidated and moved out of the upstairs portion altogether.

The Town Hall issue was widely expected to be aired at Tuesday evening's "community meeting" at the high school, a meeting that had been called to introduce the team from FEMA that would be setting up in town.

However, McCormack, who had helped set up the meeting and served as moderator, cautioned at the start that the meeting was intended to be informational only.

"It is to be hoped that people will not use the comment portion of the meeting to air their grievances," he said.

Afterwards, however, McCormack said, Selectboard Chair Neal Fox called him over and confirmed that the board still expected the Town Hall to be vacated the next day. The board also rejected, he said, the informal compromise that McCormack had proposed.

"I think they (the selectboard members) did not make the right call," he told The Herald yesterday. "They would have served the community better if they had left the clearinghouse."

Still, he noted, the selectboard has authority over use of the hall. Thus, a town hall clean-out began yesterday. Taft said she was told at noon that the town expected to have the key turned over by 5 p.m.

The proceedings yesterday were observed by a reporting team from the Valley News and a camera crew from WCAX, who had been alerted to the controversy.

> *The emergency effort was being coordinated by Amber Taft, who has worked 8-10 hours a day for three weeks, all unpaid.*

Bethel's disaster relief coordinator, Amber Taft works the phones from the Old Bethel Town Hall.

> **Hillbilly Highway ("Exit 2½") was built by Royalton residents.**

A work crew diligently removes an immense mound of silt from the Carpenter Field in South Royalton. Flooding in August left behind about three feet of muck on the athletic field, which forced South Royalton High School to play their soccer season in Randolph.

Second Branch

ROYALTON

Irene's Impact by the Numbers, *September 22*

Pam Levasseur

State Rep. Sarah Buxton has provided the following look at "Royalton by the numbers":

Eighty-nine properties affected, two major bridges crushed, four athletic fields under feet of silt and sand, 30 roads in need of repair, two schools with major damage, one Masonic temple flooded, 12 farmers suffered loss of crops, feed, or pasture, one beach "relocated", 26 homes damaged, 14 households displaced, over 900 volunteers in 10 days, 7000+ hours of volunteer labor, $25,000 raised (so far) through the support of our neighbors, one "Snakes of Ireland" benefit concert on the Green, three local churches, three schools, and dozens of businesses unified in support, one visit by Governor Peter Shumlin, two visits by Congressman Peter Welch, two federal FEMA officials in town to offer aid, one website created (http://operationreviveroyalton.com), over 1000 Facebook communications, and 114 voicemails on Rep. Buxton's cell phone.

In addition to the numbers provided by Buxton, one Hillbilly Highway ("Exit 2½") was built by Royalton residents. The unofficial highway became a main road for many, as most access roads to Royalton were heavily damaged. In part due to the amount of traffic entering the Interstate from the "Hillbilly Highway," it was closed by the Vermont State Police after only two weeks.

According to Buxton, generally, displaced families are staying with (local) friends and relatives. One family is living in a camper for a few more weeks. Three others have located to local apartments through the generosity and support of local landlords.

Dick Ellis listens to the music at the South Royalton hosted fundraising concert on the town green featuring the Snakes of Ireland.

Bill Murphy, whose home was badly damaged in the flood, sings with the local rock and blues band.

First Branch

SOUTH ROYALTON

SoRo Gets Good News on Bridges, *September 22*

Stuart Levasseur

At the September 13 meeting of the Royalton Selectboard, Chair Larry Trottier expressed thanks for everyone's efforts over the past few weeks dealing with the flood aftermath.

Jeff Tucker of DuBois and King reported on the condition of the bridges in town. The Chelsea Street bridge appears to be undamaged, he assured the board.

The Fox Stand bridge sustained significant damage to the approach, but the bridge itself was relatively unharmed, Tucker said.

The Bridge Street Bridge in Royalton village, he said, held well, also. There is once again debris under the bridge, which, due to the type of bridge it is, will need to be removed prior to use. Debris in the trusswork will interfere with the mechanics of the bridge due to tension, he noted. The northern approach is completely gone and will need to be rebuilt, but the concrete work is in good shape.

Most Roads Open

Road Foreman Roger McCrillis reported that most roads are open and at least passable.

Happy Hollow Road, however, is "a nightmare" and will not be passable for several weeks. Johnson Hill Road is still not passenger car passable. Fisher Road was reported to have difficulty with truck traffic.

Work is planned for Broad Brook Road (culvert work completed this past week).

The Mill Road bridge project has an extended completion date, now October 6 to 14 before the bridge can be opened. Gilman Road relocation is in negotiation with the landowner, and Lovejoy Road still needs attention, McCrillis said.

There are currently 14 active road projects in town due to the storm.

McCrillis also reported that the Town of Sharon has determined the bridge on lower Broad Brook will not reopen this fall/winter due to damage.

BETHEL

Kevin Michael Paquet, who works at "The Herald," and Cara Louise Tucker announced their engagement on Saturday, August 27, under the leading edge of Hurricane Irene. The happy couple is pictured here the next day on what remains of Findley Bridge Road in Bethel.

Trainloads of Rocks Head to Bethel, *October 13*

M. D. Drysdale

The need for enormous quantities of rock waste to rebuild crippled Rt. 107 has sparked a complicated network of trucks and trains to provide the required stone.

Material to reconstruct the 4.500 feet of lost roadbed is coming from some of northern New England's biggest contractors, including Whitcomb's of Colchester and Pike Industries in West Lebanon, as well as from a Pittsfield pit owned by the Harvey family.

The most spectacular and unique supply chain is the one that brings a whole trainload of rocks—some of them huge—every day via the Central Vermont Railway, dumping the rocks in the middle of Bethel village.

This is rock that starts out in a Colchester quarry, where it is carried in "big haul" truck units to Burlington to be loaded onto 15 or so railroad cars. Working around Amtrak's schedule, the railroad company can send one train to Bethel every day. The cars are especially designed to tip over and dump their contents onto a landing area.

In Bethel, that happens where the train track runs close to Peavine Boulevard, under the prominent shadow of the grain elevator on Main Street. The entire "dump car," anchored by others on each side, simply tips over and spills its load onto the side of Peavine Boulevard. It's quite a sight.

From there, the material is pushed across the road and over a bank into the property of Blossom's Firewood. At the base of the bank, the fill is loaded into more "big haul" units. These are much too big to cross the decrepit Route 107/12 bridge, so they simply drive across the White River on a fording spot that has been created.

Once across the river, the mega-trucks drive on a small road that has been built through a cornfield, ending up on River Street. From there, they turn right and head for the big washout just beyond Tozier's Restaurant on 107.

The complicated and expensive routine has raised some eyebrows in Bethel, where it's pointed out that the Rock of Ages white granite quarry has made lots of rock fill available to area towns for free.

However, according to project manager Ken Robie, the problem is not only the enormous amount of fill that's needed, but the size of the rocks themselves. Rock that will eventually hold the river bank stable can sometimes be five-foot chunks, he noted. The material is shipped by train because the "big haul" units are not allowed to travel

> *It was Irene that decided how much rock is needed—and it's a gargantuan problem.*

A train drops 15 carloads of large stones onto Peavine Boulevard in Bethel Tuesday for use as fill in the repairs of Route 107.

Julia, Michele, and Alex Robinson sort through flood-damaged golf clubs at the Renn home on Route 14 in Sharon. Karen Renn, who was still waiting for word from her insurance agent said "This isn't the worst thing that can happen to you … It's just a bump in the road and tomorrow the sun will shine."

the river as much as 20 feet or even more.

The entire Route 107 project, Robie estimated, will require more than 150,000 cubic yards of material. To put that into perspective, even the biggest of the big trucks can haul only 30 cubic yards, necessitating 5000 truck loads, or 25 trucks a day, for 200 days.

The flood-affected section of Route 107 is the "longest section of missing road" left by Irene in the whole state, said Robie. A couple of other roads were left with deeper ravines to fill, however.

So, will Route 107 be built and paved before the snow flies? Robie had a good Vermont answer:

"It depends when the snow flies," he said matter-of-factly. VTrans hopes to get all the paving done by the end of November, restoring "normal traffic" in December.

Surveying the thin line of roadbed that currently creeps along the side of the devastated river bottom, it's clear that goal will require lots more trains full of rock. The Herald asked another on-site engineer about the November 30 estimate. A smile played about his face, but he gave a straight reply.

"We'll do the very best we can," he promised.

on the Interstate. And though the Rock of Ages granite quarry is close, delivery would be difficult because of the bridge problem.

It's the contractors who make the decision of where to get the rock fill, he noted. The law of supply and demand is in full sway, and right now, "everybody needs rock," he said.

However, it was Irene that decided how much rock is needed—and it's a gargantuan problem. About 4500 linear feet of road, almost a mile, has simply disappeared, along with the roadbed itself. In some cases, the roadbed must be built up from

SHARON

River Clean-Up Day Saturday in Sharon
October 20

Since September 17, 120 volunteers have removed over three tons of trash from the White River in Hartford, Pittsfield, Rochester, and South Royalton.

There will be a river clean-up day in Sharon this Saturday, October 22 from 1-4 p.m.

Volunteers are needed to help the White River Partnership (WRP)and the town of Sharon remove post-flood debris from the banks of the White River in Sharon. Everyone is urged to meet in the town office parking lot on Route 132 at 1 p.m. to sign a waiver form and hear the safety talk. Please dress in long pants, long sleeves, and close-toed shoes or boots. Gloves, trash bags, and masks will be provided.

The clean-up is co-sponsored by the

Connecticut River Watershed Council's Source to Sea event. This fall, the WRP has helped coordinate 5 Source to Sea river clean-ups to remove debris left behind by Irene flood waters.

Since September 17, 120 volunteers have removed over three tons of trash from the White River in Hartford, Pittsfield, Rochester, and South Royalton, but more debris remains. Volunteers are invited to continue this year's river clean-up effort in Sharon in order to help the White River and landowners along the river recover from Tropical Storm Irene.

Chapter V: Afterglow

Joe Schenkman crosses over the footbridge at the junction of Routes 73 and 100 with a string bass on his way to Rochester's Harvest Festival on Saturday, September 10.

Whither the Weather

The weather is, for Vermonters, a source of infinite fascination. We talk about its impact on foliage and sugaring. We mark our lives by the blizzards and floods. We debate which road is the worst during Mud Season. We dread black ice and ice dams. Most of the world has never heard of an ice dam.

The day after Irene was the kind of summer day that sends Vermonters into a state of rapture. It was warm and sunny, the kind of day that is ideal for a float down the White River in one of those big, colorful tubes. No one was floating on this day. The river was still a snarling snake of muddy anger, filled with trees and human debris. Moreover, the river was toxic from washing over fertilized fields and liberated fuel tanks.

On Labor Day, another storm was predicted, threatening to add another five inches to a saturated land. Luckily, it turned out to be little more than an extended drizzle.

The weeks following the storm were merciful, amazingly so. There was little rain and temperatures were mild. There was no snow until a healthy dump just before Thanksgiving. Normally this would have locals exchanging thoughts on the impact on gardens and foliage. In 2011, however, the talk was on the impact on road crews and building contractors. This time, however, the news from Nature was good. The benign conditions effectively gave the carpenters, farmers, and heavy equipment operators an extra month before they had to deal with winter in addition to Irene.

Weatherwise, October 6

Kevin Doering

Although we were approaching peak leaf season, the colors were less than spectacular in the hilly portions of our area, and state foresters were reporting that saturated soils were teaming with a fungus called anthracnose, which was creating mottled patches of brown or rust amongst some of the hardwood forests in central Vermont. Elsewhere, traditional colors were more evident, including the Northeast Kingdom, which was at peak in the higher elevations along the Green Mountains to our west. Perhaps a good dry spell, with some chilly nighttime temperatures, will promote color in valley areas, which still had a way to go before reaching peak as of this writing.

After yet more damp and grey weather early this week, we were finally expected to dry out, with temperatures falling to potentially frosty conditions over the Wednesday-Thursday period, before a return to pleasantly mild weather over the weekend. Readers are advised to get out and enjoy the fall conditions, taking in the scenery, while perhaps reaching out a helping hand or two to some of our Vermont neighbors, still in need and trying to recover from the punishing floods of over a month ago.

What struck me most during this disaster, though, is the selfless dedication of volunteer fire-fighters.

Firemen Are an Inspiration

September 15 Letter to the Editor

Sue Sakai, Randolph

There are so many people to thank for coming forward and going beyond the call of duty in the wake of this epic disaster in Vermont, including private citizens, volunteer networks, private nonprofits, and government workers from FEMA and the EPA going around trying to make sure people get the assistance they need.

Perhaps what has struck me the most during this disaster, though, is the selfless dedication of volunteer firefighters in the area. John Hodgdon of Bethel and Todd Bent of Braintree in particular come to mind, but I am sure there are many others who have also gone way beyond the call of duty to keep people safe.

With that, I conclude simply by saying to the volunteer fire fighters and other emergency workers: Thank you! You are an inspiration to us all.

Agri-Mark Pays Farmers
Checks Sent Even When Milk Not Delivered, October 13

Sandy Vondrasek

Agri-Mark has paid all of its dairy farmers the full value for the milk they lost due to Tropical Storm Irene, the farm cooperative announced this week. More than 30 of the co-op's farmers throughout New England and New York were affected by the storm and could not get their milk picked up and transported to the market in a timely manner.

Two White River Valley farms, the Wright Farm on Bethel's Gilead Brook Road and Liberty Hill Farm on Route 73 in Rochester, benefited from the unanimous vote by Agri-Mark's board to issue full payment to affected farms, according to Paul Doton of Barnard, an Agri-Mark director.

Liberty Hill and the Wright Farm were among the handful of Agri-Mark farms that lost almost a week's worth of milk shipments. The cows had to be milked, but the milk was dumped.

Doton said the payments for the lost milk, generally representing several thousand dollars, was a help, but that many farms sustained severe damage, including the loss of crops and farm buildings.

Doton gave a tip of the hat to the region's milk haulers, many of whom had to drive many extra miles to pick up milk, post-Irene, and the road crews who labored overtime to restore roads.

Doton said, "The milk truck starts in Orwell and used to travel the Brandon Gap to pick up the Kennett (Liberty Hill Farm) milk and then come down the valley to Barnard."

"That day, he had to drive to Burlington, down I-89, across Route 4 and up Route 12. He never got to Kennetts at that point, and couldn't for six days."

The driver then had to drive to Brattleboro to drop off the milk, Doton said, adding "It's amazing how much got shipped."

> *Agri-Mark has paid all of its dairy farmers the full value for the milk they lost due to Tropical Storm Irene.*

The Wright farm at the top of Bethel Gilead Road was cut off from the outside until Sunday, September 4. Milk had to be dumped until then. Pictured here before the second milking on Labor Day, are Andrew, Beverly and Derrick Wright with Sam.

The White River Partnership's Greg Russ shows a culvert in Broad Brook that was temporarily replaced. The original culvert was 18" in diameter and was replaced temporarily by a 5' metal culvert, which is still three times too small for the flood volume of water. The White River Partnership hopes to have a 14' bottomless culvert installed at this site, which will prevent future blowouts and also enable fish to pass through.

On Aug. 28, tiny brooks became living monsters.

Partnership Aims at Long-Term Stream Repairs

November 3

$100,000 from Feds Will Help Prevent Culvert Blow-Outs

M. D. Drysdale

The U.S. Fish and Wildlife Service (F&W) has awarded $100,000 to the White River Partnership (WRP) to help area towns evaluate and repair washed-out culverts.

Their goal: to find out why some culverts and bridges survived the flood better than others, and to make use of that knowledge in building new ones.

The federal agency has also supplied a half-dozen or so fish passage engineers and biologists, who are eager to use their knowledge to make the next flood less devastating.

The funds will be used first to assess damages affecting stream flow and fish passage in the upper White River watershed, according to Janice Rowan, fish passage coordinator for F&W.

On August 28, tiny brooks became living monsters. The devastation observed in the upper White River watershed is particularly amazing, Rowan said, because there are examples of spectacular culvert and bridge failures almost side-by-side with unscathed culverts that were sized appropriately for fish passage.

Fish and People

"This demonstrates that what's good for fish can provide overwhelming value to humans and their safety," she said.

As a consequence, federal F&W service offered the state a hand with river management engineering and technical assistance, with the goal of helping towns pay for permanent "fish-friendly repairs," especially culverts. Professional fish passage engineers and field biologists were recruited from throughout the Northeast to provide assistance.

Trout Unlimited mobilized its membership to help provide technical assistance and oversight. The $100,000 doesn't go to the Partnership itself, stressed Mary Russ, executive director. It will be passed through to the towns to help build more effective culverts.

"The towns have been really interested in it," she said.

The fishery engineers are busy designing passages that will work for fish and withstand floods in the future. Usually, Russ noted, "more effective" culverts means "bigger" culverts, though other factors are at work.

Implementation of the culvert project will stretch into next spring "with benefits to native fish and wildlife and Vermont residents lasting much longer," Rowan concluded.

News Notes: 'Irene Recovery Moves Ahead Across Vermont,' *October 27*

M. D. Drysdale

Below are some of the statewide developments of the past week in the aftermath of Tropical Storm Irene, which devastated the state on Aug. 28.

Mobile Home Removal

Lt. Gov. Phil Scott and Secretary of Commerce and Community Development Lawrence Miller this week announced they have a plan for an affordable removal of flood-damaged mobile homes from mobile home parks in Vermont. And thanks to successful fundraising, the cost to each individual homeowner will be essentially free, they said.

It had been expected that the cost to each homeowner would be $1,500—a substantial savings over the typical removal cost of $3,500-$4,500. The group was able to achieve these savings by creating economies of scale whereby demolition contractors would work on several homes at the same location at the same time.

Thanks to an outpouring of donations after that announcement, the task force is now able to offer a $1,500 credit to each homeowner.

"With the large donations that have come in from groups like Aubuchon Hardware, the Argosy Foundation, and Ben and Jerry's, and with the help of the Vermont Community Foundation (VCF) to raise yet more funds, we're at a point where we're confident announcing that the program will, in fact, come at no cost to mobile home owners," said Secretary Miller, who worked closely with VCF on fundraising efforts.

> *"The frequency and intensity of storm activity will likely be greater during the next 100 years than it was during the last 100."*
> *Richard Tetreault*

Time To Rethink Building Bridges

Richard Tetreault, the chief engineer at Vtrans, thinks Vermont should start building differently after Irene.

On the combined town and state network, Irene washed out more than 2000 roadway segments, undermined more than 1000 culverts and damaged more than 300 bridges. The cost to rebuild everything could push $1 billion.

"Understanding that our climate is changing and that the frequency and intensity of storm activity will likely be greater during the next 100 years than it was during the last 100, it is prudent that as we rebuild we also adapt," Tetreault said.

In particular, he said, the state should reconsider bridge design.

"In the past, we built relatively short bridges with concrete abutments very close to, if not in, rushing water," he noted. "These designs were cost-effective and made environmental sense at the time.

"The time has now come, however, to consider building longer bridges with foundations that sit outside our river channels, even if these bridges cost more and have a longer footprint.

"Doing this will accommodate future flood waters, as well as allow river channels to move and not be constrained by the bridge opening and exacerbate flooding up- and downstream."

State Could Help With Abatements

Governor Shumlin, lawmakers and the Vermont League of Cities and Towns this week announced a legislative bill designed to abate some taxes for property taxpayers and towns hard-hit by Tropical Storm Irene.

Shumlin's plan would enable towns to abate education taxes for property owners hard-hit by Tropical Storm Irene and spring flooding. The plan will authorize the Tax Department to set up procedures to reimburse towns for such "extraordinary abatements."

> *Irene washed out more than 2000 roadway segments, undermined more than 1000 culverts and damaged more than 300 bridges.*

Brooklyn Bowl Fills with Vermont, *October 13*

Bob Eddy

There's nothing like the Brooklyn Bowl in Vermont, but there's one in Brooklyn, and Monday night it was all about Vermont. The popular NYC performance venue and the long-running performance artists, Blue Man Group, presented an evening benefit for "Vermont Storm Relief."

There is a strong Central Vermont connection with the New York Blue Man Group. Three performers, Brian Scott, Chris Bowen, and Isaac Eddy, all hail from the Randolph area. Eddy and Bowen performed for Monday's benefit; Scott was "bald and blue" for the Berlin show that evening. Eddy and another Vermonter, Blue Man wardrobe head, Zea Barker of Wallingford, conceived Monday's event, and then enlisted Brooklyn Bowl's manager, James Robb, committed his space and enthusiasm two weeks ago.

The Brooklyn Bowl is a huge venue. Inside the cavernous space are a blue ribbon diner, bowling alleys, a bar, a performance area, and large welcoming areas where, for this event, a showcase of Vermont products supported the cause. Donors included businesses as diverse as Burton Snowboards, Braintree's Quaker Hill Granola, and The Center for Cartoon Studies.

With the Brooklyn Bowl pledging gate receipts and Blue Man Group putting up money and huge staff support, Barker and Eddy went shopping for more corporate sponsorship and a headlining performer. Amanda Palmer, an edgy and very popular New York punk rocker in the "Brechtian" vein, and a friend of Zea Barker, readily agreed. Next, Cabot of Vermont came aboard as a major sponsor.

On stage, Palmer's talents were joined by others, including The London Souls, Sonya Kitchell, D.J. Spirit Bear and Blue Man Group. Hilarious was an impromptu Palmer/Blue Man on-stage rave with Vermont maple sugarmaker Max Cantor, from Deep Mountain Maple in West Glover.

The surprise of the evening was when Peter Yarrow, of Peter, Paul and Mary fame, took the stage and paid homage to Palmer, thanking her "for being a voice for the people, for standing in solidarity, for being here tonight." Then, magically, Yarrow and Palmer together sang "Blowin' in the Wind," and "If I had a Hammer." Said Eddy of this performance, "This was the moment in the night that made the whole event truly special. I just held my wife and sang along, watching Peter and Amanda make magic."

In addition to the donated items from Vermont, many artists donated work for the benefit. They included Brookfield's Ed Koren, who designed the poster, and numerous others including photographers Mikael Kennedy, Brian Scott, Elise Rasmussen and Bob Eddy. Original art was given by Samuel Rowlett, Alec Longtreth, Brett Haines, Amanda Palmer, and Jennifer Kahn. Darkcloud, a Vermont-born Brooklyn street artist, designed T-shirts and contributed a piece of original art. Finally, Long Trail Brewing contributed beer for the evening.

Throughout the Brooklyn Bowl—even in the bowling alley section—were movie screens, some 30 of them, showing photographs of Irene's devastation in Vermont. All of them came from the pages of *The Herald of Randolph*.

At the heart of the welcoming area, were Stuart Comstock-Gay and Scott McArdle of the Vermont Community Foundation, which has helped coordinate much of the philanthropic response following Irene.

"The energy of this evening is just incredible," said Comstock-Gay. "These people are enthusiastic, they are concerned, and they care … What's become very clear to us is that when people are given a taste of Vermont, they care about Vermont. Vermont is a beacon of inspiration and hope."

The surprise of the evening was when Peter Yarrow, of Peter, Paul and Mary fame, took the stage.

Throughout the Brooklyn Bowl—even in the bowling alley section—were movie screens, some 30 of them, showing photographs of Irene's devastation in Vermont. All of them came from the pages of The Herald of Randolph.

Peter Yarro and Amanda Palmer bring down the house with "I Had a Hammer."

Blue Man Group's Isaac Eddy of Braintree and Zea Barker of Wallingford coordinated the Brooklyn event.

Amanda Palmer revs the Brooklyn Bowl crowd for Vermont flood relief.

White River
Upper Branch

Granville

Granville Fishing Derby

Granville Roads 'Back Together,' *October 13*

Martha Slater

Granville road foreman Kevin Bagley reported that "For the most part, we're all back together, with the exception of Buffalo Hill Road, which will be closed for the winter. No one lives there during the winter, so no plowing will be done there."

Bagley said that Town Line Road has a new replacement culvert, "and that section is open one lane for now and the cement work for the head walls and wing walls and building a small retaining wall will be done before winter. We're also going to try to put more crushed gravel on all the roads that need it before winter. The bottom of Post Office will be repaved next summer, funds permitting."

Hancock

> *I sometimes think it would be nice to live in a city with shopping and lots of offerings right there, and then something like the August 28, 2011 flood happens, reminding me why I live in Hancock, VT.*

Proud of Hancock after Big Flood
September 8 Letter to the Editor

Jill Jesso-White, Hancock

I grew up hearing about the 1927 Flood from my grandfather (Andrew Jesso), but never imagined we'd have our own!

I sometimes think it would be nice to live in a city with shopping and lots of offerings right there, and then something like the August 28, 2011 flood happens, reminding me why I live in Hancock, VT. The feeling of community, family and neighbors helping neighbors has been wonderful. People have come together to help and support others. It has made us very proud and has been a great example for our daughter to witness.

Our property was hit hard, but so many others are in such worse shape that we are counting our blessings.

There are so many people and organizations that have come together during this disaster that it makes me proud to be a Vermonter. With the 10th anniversary of 9/11 this next weekend, this disaster was another important reminder about what is really important and that is family, friends, and community.

Rochester Businesses Find the Up Side to Flood; Owners Form Mutual Aid Organization In Rte. 100 Valley, *September 29*

Martha Slater

Deciding to capitalize on their success in working together in the aftermath of Hurricane Irene, an enthusiastic group of business owners from the Rochester area met Tuesday evening to form an organization to help each other and to promote the growth of business in the valley.

Hosted by Scott Holtz and Bobby Cheshire at the Huntington House, the meeting began with a potluck dinner that symbolized the group's intent—everyone contributing to the success of this new venture.

Praising the turnout that evening as "phenomenal," Holtz noted that he hoped businesses in all five towns in the valley would participate.

"We all have the same idea in that we want to work together and help each other out, and we have so much momentum after what we've just been through," he said.

"Irene put us on the map, so now we'll make lemonade out of our lemons," joked Dean Mendell, who owns several businesses in town with his wife Connie. "We need to create a business community that is welcoming."

CBS News Visits

CBS News Correspondent Wyatt Andrews and his production crew, in town while working on a segment about the flood recovery in central Vermont, joined the group for the potluck dinner and sat in on the meeting. The crew had arrived that day and filmed at the Rochester Café, the Huntington House, and Liberty Hill Farm. They planned to make a stop at the Route 73 bridge location and at work sites on Route 107 Wednesday morning.

Students in Rochester School's Art 1 class helped promote local tourism. As part of an initiative by the newly minted Green Mountain Valley Business Community, the students painted fall scenes and text onto signs that were placed throughout the area. They read "Now more than ever, thank you for visiting." Here, Carly Turnbull, left, Kira Leonard, center, and Michael Desisle work on their signs.

ROCHESTER

Local Volunteers Still Needed, *September 29*

In the aftermath of Hurricane Irene, more than 200 volunteers have traveled to help with the clean-up efforts in Rochester, Hancock, Pittsfield, and Stockbridge.

This tremendous volunteer response was recruited and organized by Cyndi Ryan and Helene Massimino, with assistance from several other local residents including the volunteer coordinators in Stockbridge and Pittsfield.

Over the last three weekends, hundreds of volunteers have shown up to help, and of this number, approximately 80% of the registered volunteers were from out-of-town and out-of-state, many traveling more than two hours to get here.

"At this point in the recovery, individuals with specialized skills such as carpentry, plumbing, and electrical are very much needed," Ryan said. "We are truly grateful to all who have responded to help since the flooding."

Crews install a temporary bridge over the Tweed River on Route 100 in Pittsfield Sunday.

Route 100 Now Fully Open, A Month After the Storm, *October 6*

The road opening came almost exactly a month after the visit of Irene on August 28.

The Vermont Agency of Transportation (VTrans) on Friday opened to public travel the 11-mile stretch of Route 100 that runs from Route 4 in Killington through Pittsfield—for 35 m.p.h. traffic. This segment of Route 100 extends to the junction of Route 107 in Stockbridge.

The road opening came almost exactly a month after the visit of Irene on August 28.

Reopening Route 100 through Pittsfield represents a major milestone because it allows the free flow of traffic without detours or major impediments for the entire 135-mile stretch of Route 100 between Ludlow and Newport just in time for the height of foliage season, VTrans noted.

Rochester T-Shirt Design Raises Awareness, $$$

October 6

Martha Slater

Seventh-generation Vermonters who grew up in Rochester, Adam Blair and his sister, Sarah Blair Durant, may live elsewhere these days, but they have an abiding love for their home state. That love inspired them to raise $26,005 (so far) for the Vermont Red Cross flood relief efforts through the sale of T-shirts and magnets that proclaim "I'm With VT," created by their family company, Independent Vermont Clothing.

The two siblings, along with their mother, Cheryl Harvey, founded Independent Vermont Clothing in September 2010, and their first sales took place at the annual Harvest Fair in Rochester that month.

Blair, who is the company's designer, said he founded IVC because he didn't like the Vermont T-shirts he saw elsewhere, "and I decided I wanted to have my own company and design shirts that I would wear."

Blair lives in Washington, D.C., where he works as a photographer and editor for the British network Independent Television News. A 1997 graduate of Rochester High School, he graduated from RIT in 2001 and began his career in television news with WCAX-TV in Burlington. After living and working in California for a few years, he returned to the east coast last year, and travels all over the world as part of his job.

In the past year, he's covered stories in Haiti and Libya, followed Prince William and his new bride across Canada, and covered the 10th anniversary of 9/11 in New York City. He was in New York covering Hurricane Irene when he discovered how hard it had hit his home state.

"I came up with a design and we started taking orders for T-shirts to benefit the Vermont Red Cross by 9 a.m. on August 30," Blair said Tuesday, October 4 as he and family members worked busily to fill orders at the command center in the kitchen of his mother's home on Route 100.

"We thought we could raise about $500. We were used to getting several orders a month, but all of a sudden when we put the shirt on our Facebook page and sent e-mails out to our friends, things went wild.

"Our web site exploded with as many as 10,000 hits on our busiest day, and by our order deadline of October 1, we had sold 1,800 'I'm With VT' shirts. By that final day of taking orders, we had raised $26,005 from the shirts and magnets."

Orders came in from 45 states, as well as Italy, England, Ireland, Australia, Canada, and other countries.

> *"When we put the shirt on our Facebook page and sent e-mails out to our friends, things went wild."*
> *Adam Blair*

> "There seems to be a consensus that our product here is peace and quiet—we just need to communicate what it is we have to offer."
> Doon Hinderyck

Damaged contents from a flooded basement in Rochester

Green Mountain Valley Business Community Gets to Work, *October 20*

The newly formed Green Mountain Valley Business Community met Tuesday, Oct. 11 at the Village Porch, with 20 members present.

Since most of those at the meeting were from Rochester, they talked about how to attract members from all five towns so those towns would all feel like they were a part of the group.

A mission statement committee was formed, with Valerie Levitan, Larry Pleasant, Scott Holtz, Julia Purdy, and Barb Harvey volunteering to serve as members. Dean Mendell pointed out that people who own small businesses in the area are "used to doing their own thing, and it will be good for us to work together."

"There seems to be a consensus that our product here is peace and quiet—we just need to communicate what it is we have to offer," said Doon Hinderyckx.

> *To date, the committee has disbursed approximately $105,465 to 36 families and individuals.*

Rochester Relief Committee News, *November 3*

The Rochester Relief Committee continues to meet weekly to review grant applications for flood relief. To date, the committee has disbursed approximately $105,465 to 36 families and individuals. That amount includes 13 grants for debris removal totaling $10,965; urgent need grants totaling $15,000; and close to $79,500 in larger flood relief grants. The largest grants were made to those whose homes were destroyed or significantly damaged by the flood.

The committee will continue to make grants to flood victims as funds allow, and the members encourage and appreciate further donations that enable them to assist neighbors in their recovery. Donations can be made either to Relief for Rochester or the Rebuild Rochester Foundation. Both funds are fully described on the town website: rochestervermont.org.

White River Valley Players Present Original Songs, Plays About 'Irene,' *November 3*

The White River Valley Players will present "More Than Gravel Was Stirred," newly-written songs and short plays by local writers, all inspired by experiences during Tropical Storm Irene, Friday and Saturday, November 11 and 12 at 7:30 p.m. and Sunday, November 13 at 2 p.m. at the Park House on Main Street in Rochester.

The Players' "home," the Rochester High School auditorium, was heavily damaged by the record-breaking storm, and the 30-year-old community theater group has taken on the project of fundraising to replace the hundreds of seats that had to be removed. All proceeds from ticket sales for this show will be used for that special "Save a Seat!" fund.

The plays and songs that will be presented are the result of workshops held after the flood. The playwrights include Ginny Scott-Bowman, Ethan Bowen, Monica Collins, Amy Braun, and Susie Smolen. Songwriters are Dorothy Robson, Susan Rule, Sue Clarke, Chelsea Lowe, Leslie Blair, and Jeanie Levitan Crickard.

"These performances are a creative, positive response and result of the trying things that Tropical Storm Irene left for our community to deal with," said the show's producer, Ginny Scott-Bowman. "Our community pulled together and worked together and turned a bad thing into a good thing. We are using the Park House to present this show, since it is more intimate, and all the plays and songs are original."

> *"Our community pulled together and worked together and turned a bad thing into a good thing."*
> *Ginny Scott*

Pittsfield Shows How To Work Together

September 22

Howard Gunter

On Sunday, August 28, 2011, Hurricane Irene ravaged the East Coast of the United States, and the town of Pittsfield became an instant island.

To panic would be an understandable reaction, but panic was not to be found in Pittsfield. By daylight Monday, August 29, rumbling noises were heard all around as farmers, and equipment owners joined the ranks of the town highway department. The town selectboard and administration swung into action without any hesitation.

Recovery had begun!

The fire department and first responders mobilized on off-road vehicles, tractors and on foot to immediately check on the entire population with emphasis on those families trapped, stranded or otherwise at risk. Everyone was accounted for and, if needed, relocated to safe housing. Local inns and larger homes became sanctuaries for those who were now homeless.

Pittsfield is home to one of the area's major fuel supply companies, so propane and fuel oil would be readily available. Merchants handed out ice and water from their inventories. The one gas station wisely began rationing gas at a five-gallon maximum to be used for generators only. Those who had generators began rotating them among neighbors for a few hours at a time to help with maintaining refrigerators and freezers.

The town constables instituted safety and security measures from the start. Initially, town meetings were held every other day at 7:30 a.m. so that everyone could remain informed as to recovery progress and vital information to help themselves and their neighbors. Meetings were held in the local church.

This story is about hometown heroes.

Tweed River

PITTSFIELD

Howard Gunter

Focus on Community

The theme of "Community" became the focus for all. The best thing that a family could do was to take best care of themselves and then reach out to immediate neighbors. It wasn't long before restoration of friendships became a regular occurrence. Squabbles and differences fell into embraces and tears of apologies and forgiveness. Our community became a "Community" in every sense of the word. A wedding took place in the midst of the hustle and bustle of a town digging its way out.

Too Many To Mention

This story is about hometown heroes, and names are not mentioned because everyone in town played a big part and it would be an injustice to omit even one. Many of our local men worked 10, 12 and more hours, day after day, with heavy equipment, tractors and shovels.

Town administrators worked into the night every day making sure that coordination with outside agencies and government entities was properly recorded and in place. Oversight of the emergency processes and genuine care for Pittsfield kept them busy.

One local fund is established to receive donations and administer financial assistance: pittsfieldhurricanerelief.org is a primary means of being assured that all donations collected will go directly to victims.

Our community became a "Community" in every sense of the word.

All the kids from the Barstow Memorial School in Chittenden were lining the lawn in front of the school to wave to us, waving flags and clapping.

Sotirakis, Chittenden F. D. Work Tirelessly To Help Pittsfield Bounce Back, *October 20*

Martha Slater

Ever since Hurricane Irene arrived in Vermont, and particularly in Pittsfield, Jan Sotirakis has been on a mission.

For almost two months, she and her fellow members of the Chittenden Volunteer Fire Department have worked countless hours to help flood victims in her old hometown. Since Chittenden suffered only minor flood damage, the folks there decided to help others who weren't so fortunate.

Raised in Pittsfield, Sotirakis lived there until she was 21, but now lives in Chittenden. She's a retired nurse who worked for the state for 32 years, the last 17 doing district emergency planning preparedness for the Rutland district office of the health department.

"The day after the flood I was going crazy, because I couldn't find a place that needed my skills to help," she said.

After her nephew Josh Merrill, who grew up in Stockbridge but now lives in Rutland, started sharing information with her from his Facebook contacts about how much damage this area sustained, she found her mission.

The fire department opened an emergency operation center in Chittenden Wednesday, August 31 and Sotirakis took to the airwaves, asking for donations on local radio stations. They started to pour in, and on the first day, they had enough items so that, at noon, four truckloads were ready to be delivered into Pittsfield.

Since they were classified as emergency vehicles and providing essential service, Sotirakis said they could get clearance to go every day at noon on Route 4 in a caravan with one of the fire department trucks leading and every truck bearing an American flag to make them identifiable.

"On the third day of our operation to help Pittsfield, we took out 11 loads," she recalled. "All the kids from the Barstow Memorial School in Chittenden were lining the lawn in front of the school to wave to us, waving flags and clapping. That's when it first really hit us that

'It's All About Neighbors Helping Neighbors'

what we were doing was important and meaningful." After that, they learned very quickly that the road crew, the National Guard, and the sheriff's department were their friends, and if they followed the rules, they would have access to the roads when they needed to.

"We brought them cookies, brownies, bottled water and fresh apples so they would have snacks while they were working," Sotirakis said. "As soon as they saw us coming through, they would give us the thumbs up. Local Chittenden people baked the cookies and brownies and put them in Ziploc bags for us."

The department's original intent was to provide services to Pittsfield, but the next day, they got a request for help from Stockbridge. On September 1, they delivered three loads to Stockbridge and eight to Pittsfield, including cleaning supplies, bottled water, food for both people and pets, baby supplies, and personal care items. On September 12, a truckload went to Rochester, and others went to Hancock, Killington, Mendon, and

Bridgewater—120 loads in all in 15 days.

"At one point," Sotirakis recalled, with a laugh, "we had a request for fresh meat for Pittsfield and I handed my personal credit card to a complete stranger (a few other people in the station knew her) and gave her my PIN number and asked her to go to Price Chopper to get $500 worth of hamburger. She came right back with it. Everyone was so helpful!"

"Once the towns didn't need any more food supplies and road access was becoming available, we went through withdrawal—what do we do now?" she said. "We decided that we weren't going to stop. We wouldn't ask for any more food, but we would ask for financial donations to help those who needed to rebuild."

"The reactions of the families that we've given money to have been wonderful," she said. "We've gotten some incredible thank you notes from people who are amazed that complete strangers want to help them. Some have even said 'Where IS Chittenden?' For me, it's all about neighbors helping neighbors."

> *"I handed my personal credit card to a complete stranger and gave her my pin number and asked her to go to Price Chopper to get $500 worth of hamburger."*
> *Jan Sotirakis*

Pittsfield Flood Recovery Report: Town Roads Now in 'Decent Shape,' *October 6*

Martha Slater

Interviewed via phone Tuesday, Oct. 4, Pittsfield Town Clerk Patty Haskins reported, "The good news from Pittsfield is that our town highways are now in decent shape, thanks to our town road crew and local contractors. They did a great job. Much of the emergency work is done and they are now getting ready to start the more permanent work—continuing to install culverts, ditching, putting a top coat of gravel on, bank stabilization, etc. Our road foreman, George Deblon, is trying to get them ready for winter. The Army Corps of Engineers also worked on debris removal from the rivers."

Haskins praised the efforts of the town's emergency operations coordinator, Peter Borden, who "worked with both the town and state road crews and the Army crew, and coordinated the entire effort with setting up a medical clinic. He also worked with constables and basically coordinated everything!"

For the most part, people here have gone somewhat back to their normal lives," she said, "but for the people who had significant damage to their homes or were completely displaced, it's a very different world for them now. We must make sure we continue to work to meet their needs and take care of them."

Haskins said that all the town's displaced people are temporarily in other locations. There were a total of eight families permanently displaced by the flooding in Pittsfield.

"Pastor Howard Gunter of the Pittsfield Federated Church is working with people who have particular needs and matching them with folks donating items they might need," Haskins added. "The website pittsfieldhurricanerelief.org is also helping to meet the needs of local people. We're also fortunate to have the Chittenden Volunteer Fire Department continue to look after us here and fundraise on behalf of people here and throughout the White River Valley."

> *There were a total of eight families permanently displaced by the flooding in Pittsfield.*

Completion Date Set for Riford Brook Bridge
October 20

Sandy Vondrasek

A contract has been awarded for the reconstruction of the Riford Brook Road bridge in Braintree, and the project is due to be "substantially finished" by November 15.

Holly Jarvis, administrative assistant to the Braintree Selectboard, reported this week that preparatory work for the project, including removal of guardrails, began this week.

The Braintree Selectboard, which moved quickly, post-Irene, to get an engineering plan for the bridge repair, awarded a $347,000 contract for the project two weeks ago to Vermont Siteworks of Morrisville.

Flooding on August 28 washed out a big section of the western approach to the bridge, leaving the concrete abutment standing, isolated, on its cylindrical support piers.

Engineering plans call for a quantity of "flowable fill," a concrete-like substance, to be poured around that abutment, Jarvis said. A huge amount of rock and fill will then be trucked in to replace what Irene washed downstream, and, finally, the road surface leading to the western end of the deck will be rebuilt.

Engineers have determined that the bridge deck itself is "just fine," Jarvis said.

The loss of the bridge has created transportation headaches for residents of the road since the flooding.

School buses are still not going down the road, Jarvis said. The total cost to repair flood-damaged roads and bridges in Braintree is presently estimated at about $1 million, according to Jarvis.

Third Branch

Braintree

Riford Brook Road: Drive to 12A
Just Got Faster, *November 10*

The students and working folks of Riford Brook Road no longer have to scramble up and down ladders—or drive the long way around—to get to school or work.

The bridge approach on the eastern end of the road, badly damaged by the flood, is again open. Vermont Siteworks completed the project last Friday, November 4.

"It's wonderful," commented long-time Riford Brook resident Stella Flint this week. "It was hard for the working women on the road, who have been climbing ladders for two months."

The rebuilt bridge approach will be blacktopped this week, she said.

> *"It was hard for the working women on the road, who have been climbing ladders for two months. "*
> *Stella Flint*

Local Fundraisers Net $32K for Irene Victims

October 13

Sandy Vondrasek

Evidently, a lot of people were just looking for a way to help their neighbors. Three recent fundraisers in the Randolph area—a September 30 pig roast, an October 1 spaghetti dinner and silent auction, and a tag sale over the Columbus Day weekend—raised more than $32,000, all to benefit local victims of Irene's wrath.

Most phenomenally successful was the combined spaghetti dinner, silent auction and dance at the Braintree Town Hall, which raised more than $24,000 for flood victims in Braintree, West Braintree, East Granville, and Roxbury.

A good portion of the funds came in at the event itself, with the balance from checks sent to the Braintree Town Clerk's office. Checks are still coming in—and can still be sent, said organizer Shirley Hook.

Advertising for the fund drive/fundraiser noted that an anonymous donor had pledged to give $5000, if that much could be raised.

In the end, the mystery donor sent in a check for $6000, and a number of other local residents sent in "very generous checks," Hook noted.

Hook and her husband Doug Bent were the prime movers for the big bash, but they had plenty of help, she emphasized. Chief among them were Mary Merusi, and Rick and Sherri Grant. Hook said many local businesses donated items for the silent auction and for the meal. A donated Vermont Castings grill did double-duty, fundraising-wise, as the winner of the raffle donated it back.

Hook said the grill was then sold for $1500, with all of the proceeds added to the substantial fund, established under the Town of Braintree's non-profit designation.

Pig Roast

"Well, basically, Randolph went hog wild," was Rev. Ron Rilling's tongue-in-cheek assessment of a September 30 benefit pig roast at Green Mountain Gospel Chapel. The event cleared more than $4000 for local flood relief.

"We expected maybe a couple hundred people; we prepared for 325, because I always plan for more; and 400-and-something showed up," Rev. Rilling said. "It was absolutely overwhelming."

It was also a fun night for everybody, as diners lingered on in the big tent until after 9 p.m. to visit and enjoy music performed by a variety of individuals and groups.

Like Hook, Rilling expressed his thanks to local merchants who donated tems for the event.

Rilling said a portion of the funds raised will go to the Randolph Area Food Shelf, and options are still being explored for the balance. "We're talking to Central Vermont Community Action; we have a couple of different ideas," he said.

One of the ideas, Rilling said, is to send teams of workers out to re-insulate homes that had to be gutted due to flood damage. Bethel Mills has agreed to provide a big discount on insulation, he said.

That way, he said, "rather than just giving the money out, we would actually have a part in helping."

Tag Sale

Lee Khan of Brookfield, who spearheaded last weekend's October 8-10 tag sale in Randolph, said the event cleared more than $4000. The sale, in a big tent outside Riches Recycled, Route 12S, was part fundraiser and part "community service," in that flood victims were invited to take anything they needed for free. As advertised, tag sale proceeds will go to David Atkinson of Braintree, who lost his home to Riford Brook on August 28.

Khan gave special tribute to Irene Shaefer of Randolph, who recruited and scheduled volunteers. "She had volunteers for sorting, pricing, selling, to pick up tables, and to pick up bigger donated items. We had 15 volunteers just in close-down today," Khan said, adding, "We called her 'Irene-Not-the-Hurricane'—she got it all organized."

> *The sale, was part fundraiser and part "community service," in that flood victims were invited to take anything they needed for free.*

David Atkinson managed to walk out of the isolated Riford Brook area of Braintree to get a warm breakfast at The Three Bean Cafe in Randolph, Tuesday morning, August 30.

'Thank You' Isn't Adequate
November 13 Letter to The Editor

David Atkinson, Braintree

I have been using words to express myself for 70 years. Since Columbus Day Weekend I have been trying to find the words to express my gratitude for the overwhelming and heartwarming support I have received from the people of this area.

The outpouring of donations and the number of people who bought things at the five-day yard sale in Randolph remain forever etched in my mind.

I feel very fortunate to live in Vermont and to be a part of this community.

I have always enjoyed giving, and it is very humbling to be on the receiving end of the gift you gave me.

I hope to live long enough to give back the kindness I have received from you. Till then, I must resort to these simple two words. Thank you.

Town Employees' Quick Action Rescued Five Buses from the Flood, *September 29*

Sandy Vondrasek

One month after Irene pummeled Vermont, stories and images from that day continue to arrive at *The Herald.*

This startling picture was forwarded to the paper by Brent Kay, superintendent of the Orange Southwest Supervisory Union. It had recently been shown to him, Kay said, by Wes Gibbs, OSSU's transportation coordinator.

"You can see the buses in the background are in deep trouble, and it would not have been much longer before the water level reached the engines, inner compartments, radios, and seats," Supt. Kay wrote in an email.

The photo was taken just before 3 p.m. on Sunday, August 28, when water levels along the Third Branch suddenly surged higher.

Thanks to quick action by three Town of Randolph employees, the five buses that had been parked off Hedding Drive, near the town garage, were driven to safety just in the nick of time.

The rescuers were John Coffey, chief operator of the water and sewer systems, Highway Supervisor Rob Runnals, and Bill Morgan, the town's buildings, grounds, and highway operations manager.

"It is without question that if these people had not proactively helped us out, a significant portion of our bus fleet would have been lost," Kay noted. "The cost to our taxpayers would have been in the hundreds of thousands of dollars."

A new bus costs $80,000-$100,000, he noted.

RANDOLPH

Baseball Event Raises More Than $200,000
For Farmers Devastated by Irene, *November 17*

Stephen Morris

For one night Randolph Center was the epicenter of the baseball universe.

Buster Olney became the stuff of local legend–at least in the eyes of his teammates on the Mets of the Randolph Little League–when he dared to throw a 15-foot-high "eephus" pitch in an actual game. That was circa 1976. Now, he is the stuff of local legend as he has gone on to national prominence as a writer and broadcast journalist. Late last summer when he posted photos on his blog of the damage done to local farms by Tropical Storm Irene, Brian Cashman, general manager of the Yankees, responded immediately, saying "You've got to do something, and if you do, I'll be there."

A total of 463 farms in Vermont were impacted by the storm, suffering more than $20 million in damages with more than 10,000 acres affected.

The media descended on Judd Hall at VTC at 4:00 in the afternoon. There was Cashman, surrounded by reporters; there was Huntington; but the question on everyone's mind was whether Theo Epstein would actually show. His commitment was made before the biblical collapse of the Red Sox in September, an event that, in turn, triggered a succession of events that included the departure of Red Sox manager Terry Francona, and Epstein accepting a new position as President of Baseball Operations with the Cubs. With all the turmoil of a new job and commuting between Chicago and his family in Boston, would Epstein, who earned the reputation as a rock star baseball executive by virtue of ending the "curse of the Bambino", actually show up in Randolph Center?

Suddenly, there he was. Trim, tall, immaculately dressed and coiffed, Epstein looked the part of baseball royalty. At a pre-event "meet and greet" at the new VTC student center, Epstein was patient and gracious as he shook hands, posed for pictures, and smiled as a stream of star-struck fans mumbled thank yous for the World Championships and best wishes for the new job in Chicago.

From left to right: Red Sox scout Galen Carr, Yankees GM Brian Cashman, Cubs GM Theo Epstein, Pirates GM Neal Huntington, and ESPN's Buster Olney.

> "I'll be there. "
> **Theo Epstein**

This event benefited not only the baseball fans of Vermont, but the state's community of farmers. In his blog, Olney estimates that at least $175,000 will be raised for the farmers. The participating baseball celebrities deserve thanks for their gracious generosity, and the event organizers should be congratulated for the ultimate feel-good event. When the crowd had gone home, and the stands were empty, however, Vermont farmers still have a long way to fully recover from Irene.

Randolph Center farmer and "Going To Bat for Vermont Farmers" co-organizer, Sam Lincoln, stands behind a World Series trophy at Saturday's VTC event.

A Call from Sam Lincoln

Three days after the event, Sam Lincoln was still on an adrenaline high. "I'll be writing thank-you notes until Christmas," he said. A total of 613 tickets were sold for the event, ranging from $20 for a bleacher seat to $250 for the VIP reception. Lincoln confirmed that everything had gone perfectly. $160,000 raised to date, with $200,000 within sight.

"After the event, Buster and I went home, and we were too excited to go to sleep. We stayed up half the night talking."

Lincoln said his feedback from the celebrity panelists was so positive that "I think they got as much out of it as everyone else." When Olney walked Theo Epstein to his car, Epstein reportedly said "I've been to a lot of these kinds of events, and this one is as good as it gets."

Epstein was so enthusiastic about his Vermont experience that he doubled his donation for a "meet and greet" for four people at Wrigley Field this next summer.

Some notable winning auction items from Sunday's first round: Ozzie Smith Wheaties box $125; Mike Barnicle's four Row A seats at Fenway next to the dugout $4,515; Toby Keith concert tickets with a backstage meet and greet $2,100; Albert Pujols autographed baseball $341; Carlton Fisk autographed bat $325; a day with a baseball agent at Fenway $1,550; National Baseball Hall of Fame behind-the-scenes tour $1,470 and the Buster Olney tour of ESPN $1,575.

"There are so many people to thank. If I can boil the experience down to one word, it's 'gratitude'."

Flood Help in Bethel Gilead

September 9 Letter to the Editor

Tom and Barbara Pinello, Bethel Gilead

During Hurricane Irene, Bethel Gilead, like so many other areas, was hit very hard.

Sunday afternoon: our brook rose suddenly and took out our bridge and road. The rest of our valley was even more heavily damaged. We were isolated and without power and phone until Friday evening.

We want to express how very grateful we are to our family, our neighbors and friends; and the Bethel road crew that worked long hours every day to make the road passable.

We were overwhelmed by so many volunteers—neighbors and strangers—who came to our house to be sure we were safe, did errands, and provided support at a very difficult time.

Barbara Pinello

Chuck Cacciatore of Castleton snaps a shot of himself and his son, Charlie 13, with the Yankees' World Series trophy during the "Going To Bat for Vermont Farmers" fundraiser.

BETHEL

David Aldrighetti, Bethel
Fire Department Chief

Just Too Many Folks to Thank

September 22 Letter to the Editor

*Many times we
would get back to
our station after
putting in up to
16 hours a day
to find a warm
meal all set up
and waiting.*

*David Aldrighetti, Chief,
Bethel Fire Department*

Last Monday night, the Bethel Fire Department had its first department meeting since Hurricane Irene hit.

Many members of our department put in over 100 hours, starting from flooded roads Sunday the 28th , through washing out our local businesses on the 12th , plus doing everything else that had to be done in between, including swift water rescues/fire calls/home evacuations to traffic control!

After cleaning up and putting all our equipment back in order, the first subject that came up was how to thank all the people who helped us through the last couple weeks. I was humbled by the fact that as we discussed who we needed to be giving thanks to, the list just went on and on. We decided the only way to cover all of them was just one big "THANK

YOU" to all of you who helped.

The community stepped in and assisted us day after day with food, water, supplies, or anything we needed. Many times we would get back to our station after putting in up to 16 hours a day to find a warm meal all set up and waiting for us, or standing outside helping the highway crew for 12 hours and having meals delivered to us was the boost that kept us all going!

To see such community support shows how strong we can all be in such heartbreaking times. The only personal thank-you I would like to say is to all of my fellow fireman and their families from our community as well as our neighboring communities for sacrificing their own personal time in order to give to others. It's a true sign of how strong we can be when we are needed the most!

So again, to all of you, "THANK YOU."

Earthmovers work to restore the White River.

Bethel's Athletic Field is immersed in floodwater.

> *One of the more heartwarming responses to Tropical Storm Irene has been the creation of a sort of Youth Soccer Central in Kellogg's hayfield.*

Flooded Out and Relocated, Youth Soccer Lives On, *October 20*

M. D. Drysdale

Saturday drivers on Route 12 between Bethel and Randolph may be startled to see a soccer game going on in Tom Kellogg's farm field across the road from Onion Flats.

Then they will spy a second game, and a third, and fourth—and more.

One of the more heartwarming responses to Tropical Storm Irene has been the creation of a sort of Youth Soccer Central in Kellogg's hayfield. After flood waters covered all of Bethel's soccer fields and some of Randolph's, Corey Stearns, as head of Bethel Youth Soccer, got permission from Kellogg to play soccer there. Then, Jeff Townsend, who was renting the fields, agreed to cut his hay early, in the middle of the night, to make room for soccer.

Stearns got in touch with his Randolph counterpart, Matt Murawski, and the two of them, along with Corey's father Dennis, mowed and lined the fields. Goals for seven fields were created out of plastic pipe donated by Lucky's and fabricated for free by Mark Nicholson.

Now, on Saturday mornings, and Tuesdays and Thursdays too, Kellogg's field is alive with kids, from kindergarteners through sixth grade, directed by a dozen or so volunteer coaches. There are dozens upon dozens of kids, from South Royalton and Rochester as well as Bethel and Randolph. Stearns noted that the Bethel program alone serves 75 to 90 children.

Having a Ball

Soccer as far as the eye can see fills a dozen fields along Route 12 on Onion Flats each Saturday morning.

The youngest participants in Area Youth Soccer show their abundant enthusiasm before taking to the field.

Running hard (and maybe a jacket, or two) helps keep the brisk autumn at bay.

Bethel Area Flood Victims Received New Free Clothing, *October 20*

Amy Danley-White

On the morning of Saturday, October 12, a festive atmosphere could be found under the Bethel Elementary School canopy. A large truck dispensed free clothing, while the Bethel Area Rotary Club gave away hot drinks and pastries, and Spencer Lewis played the fiddle. The reason for the event was not so merry, though, since the giveaway was to provide area flood victims with some much-needed warm clothing.

Karen Speerstra of Sophia Serve in Randolph Center, has networked with St. Paul's Episcopal Church in White River Junction, Christ Church in Bethel, and Lenny's Shoes in Barre to distribute Carhartt clothing and Red Wing boots to area flood victims. This is part of a statewide effort to make sure flood victims have warm winter clothes.

Speerstra said that she had worked with Bethel Town Manager Dell Cloud and Assistant Manager Abbie Sherman to get a list of Bethel residents affected by Hurricane Irene. The list showed eight businesses, 75 private dwellings, and nine mobile homes damaged in the flood. The church volunteers made calls to all parties on the list to let them know about the clothing giveaway.

$6.4 Million Bridge for Bethel, *October 20*

M. D. Drysdale

The River Street Bridge in Bethel survived Tropical Storm Irene, just barely, but it's being replaced anyway.

Construction is already underway to prepare for a new $6.4-million bridge, which should be ready next fall to handle the heavy traffic on combined Routes 12 and 107. The new bridge will be very similar to the current bridge, according to resident engineer Jeremy Reed, although it will be somewhat wider, with an 11-foot travel lane, three-foot shoulders, and a 5.5-foot sidewalk.

The new bridge will duplicate the existing high iron truss arrangement. It's the sort of bridge you don't see built new very often, and is more expensive than a

"normal" bridge placed on girders. Reed said it became apparent early on that girders would not be acceptable at this location. Deep girders would leave less capacity for river flow under the bridge (the "hydraulic opening"), he explained.

Previous versions discussed included a long "bypass" bridge from the other end of River Street over both the river and railroad, and even a duplication of the pre-1904 covered bridge.

The covered bridge was replaced in 1904 with a steel truss bridge, which washed out during the 1927 Flood, he said. The current span was built in 1928, a year in which more bridges were built in Vermont than in any year before or since.

> *The current span was built in 1928, a year in which more bridges were built in Vermont than in any year before or since.*

Early the morning of August 29 – Bethel's 1928 iron bridge had survived Irene.

Repairs to Bethel Gilead Brook Road continued throughout November.

Good Job, Bethel, On Our Roads

October 20 Letter to the Editor

Ann M. Johnson, Bethel

I would like to sincerely thank the Bethel town manager, select-board and our town road crew for their efforts in reconnecting, as quickly as possible, those of us who live in the hills surrounding Bethel, to the rest of the world in the aftermath of Tropical Storm Irene.

Putting "Band-Aids" on our roads within hours of the storm made it possible for the utility companies to get to us and restore power and telephone service. Many of us did not have water, as we depend on wells and the efforts of the volunteers who navigated their way over treacherous terrain on their ATVs to bring water and supplies to us were a godsend.

Generally those of us who live in the hills are prepared for severe snow storms and usually have back-up food and water at all times during the winter months as we are, after all, responsible for our own well-being and survival. However, Irene left a lot of us flat-footed in that respect, as no one would have ever expected a totally debilitating storm like Irene at this time of the year.

There are many of us who appreciate your time, dedication and efforts when we needed you most.

New Life for Peavine Park, *October 27*

Among the many devastating legacies of Irene was the one to three feet of silt deposited on Peavine Park in Bethel. The park is a much beloved spot in the town of Bethel, for picnicking, recreation, and access to the Third Branch of the White River. Established in 1991 by the Bethel Business Association, it was a gift from the Gaiko family.

When October 22 was officially declared "Vermont Clean-Up Day" by Governor Peter Shumlin, Preserve Peavine became just one of the many projects taking place in Vermont that day. The mission of the Peavine project included digging out the gazebo, water fountain, several memorial benches, and cedar fences. In addition, the silt needed to be pulled away from around the bases of the many trees in the park. All this work was necessary to allow the town of Bethel to efficiently use large equipment to continue the removal of the silt this fall so the park can return to life next spring.

Lisa Campbell sent out word via the Vermont Clean-Up Day website, and social media, about the planned event to work on the site. In response, over 50 volunteers descended on the park to start the painstaking work of digging it out. Among those who turned up, shovels in hand, were a number of local folks, as well as volunteers from Congressman Welch's office, Community College of Vermont, St. Michael's College, Champlain College, and the University of Vermont. UVM'ers

> *The mission of the Peavine project included digging out the gazebo, water fountain, several memorial benches, and cedar fences.*

As lunchtime approached, the first order of business for volunteers at Peavine Park was to dig the park benches out from the silt. The thick muck made for a handy footrest.

Governor Peter Shumlin lends a hand Saturday at Peavine Park cutting limbs with a chainsaw.

also worked at Riverside Mobile Home Park in West Woodstock and at several sites in Rochester. The university's Clean-Up Day contingent of about 80 volunteers was one of the largest in the state.

Several young people from the mentor organization, The Dream Program, also added their efforts to the Peavine mission. Newall and Barbara Wood joined the group and provided some of the history of the park. Bethel Town Manager Dell Cloud arranged for a front-end loader and driver to assist in the day's activities. Bill Brainard volunteered his dump truck for the purpose of moving silt from the park's parking lot. Both Governor Peter Shumlin and Congressman Peter Welch assisted in the efforts of the group.

The Bethel Rotary Club and Rebbie Carleton provided morning coffee, snacks, and lunch for the group.

New Relief Center Has Goods for Flood Victims in Region, *October 27*

Sandy Vondrasek

A new flood relief center in Bethel is operating out of the former Richardson's Store site on Main Street, with a collection of material goods for flood victims in the area. Bethel resident Ola O'Dell, the driving force behind "Bethel's Irene Recovery and Renew Center," said this week that the project has received some notable donations of both new and used goods.

"This is to serve the region," O'Dell said. "It's not strictly limited to Bethel residents. It's for anybody who was flooded out and who needs help. Winter is coming and we have lots of winter things."

O'Dell said the Richardson family offered free use of the vacant storefront, in exchange for giving the space a thorough cleaning. As part of the deal, O'Dell also scrubbed and polished furniture that belongs to the Masons. The furniture, which had been in a flooded building, was later moved to Richardson's.

Some of the volunteers who came to Bethel Saturday, as part of the statewide volunteer effort, helped to set up the space, O'Dell said.

The Richardson family offered free use of the vacant storefront, in exchange for giving the space a thorough cleaning.

Ola O'Dell, the driving force behind "Bethel's Irene Recovery and Renew Center," scrubs and polishes the vacant storefront for opening.

Paving Work on Bethel Mountain Road Done in Time for Winter

Martha Slater

As a result of flooding from Hurricane Irene, large stretches of the lower portion of Bethel Mountain Road/Camp Brook Road (what you call it depends on which side of the mountain you live on) that connects Rochester and Bethel were severely damaged or in some spots, destroyed.

In the more than two months since the storm, the town road crew from Bethel has put in many long hours working to repair and rebuild the road. Just last week, the repaired sections were repaved, resulting in widespread rejoicing (and a much smoother trip) for the many folks who drive over that road every day.

Bethel town manager Dell Cloud told The Herald that the town road crew had done all of the restoration and prep work, including replacing several culverts and literally rebuilding the roadbed, which had to be filled in with boulders and rip rap. In some places, there were 15-foot deep chasms.

"We had 65% of our roads that were destroyed," Cloud explained, "but that's certainly been the most costly portion per mile to repair. Pretty much every one of those roads will be in usable order by winter and the final repairs will be made next year."

Bethel Volunteer Fire Department Headed to Fenway, November 24

Stephen Morris

Green Monstah, here we come!

The people of Bethel don't see eye-to-eye on all issues, but they seem to find common ground when it comes to recognizing the solid (some would say "heroic") performance of the town's volunteer fire department. In April, 2012, that recognition will be shared with the entire Red Sox Nation when the group will be honored in a pre-game ceremony at Fenway Park.

The firefighters were gathered on Monday, November 21 for their bi-weekly meeting. Usually the agenda consists of announcements by the chief (David Aldrighetti), followed by training and equipment inspection. This night, however, they are waiting for the phone to ring.

"It seemed like the Bethel firefighters were everywhere just after the storm," says Sam Lincoln in a pre-meeting phone call. Lincoln has been in the news of late for his role as one of the principal organizers in the Going to Bat for Vermont fundraiser that netted $200,000 to help Vermont farmers recover from the damages caused by Irene. Now Lincoln, accompanied by his son in a Red Sox T-shirt, is sitting with the firefighters, waiting for the phone to ring.

The phone rings.

Aldrighetti answers, hands the phone to Lincoln, who–after a few pleasantries–says "Hold on, I'm putting this is Sam Kennedy of the Boston Red Sox." Kennedy is Chief Operating Officer. "I heard from your friend Buster Olney what a fantastic job you all did during the recent storm, and we'd like you to be our guests at a game next April and to be honored in a pre-game ceremony on the field."

The call is brief, followed by robust applause. Afterwards, Aldrighetti and Lincoln add some administrative details ("We're going to hire a bus and make a day of it." "These tickets are non-transferable." Wouldn't want these showing up on eBay.) Most in attendance, however, are picturing themselves in the shadow of the Green Monstah, their faces up on the Jumbotron screen. For any kid raised in New England, it will be a dream come true.

The siren wails into the November night, normally a call of alarm. Tonight, however, the fire fighters are already gathered. Tonight, the siren is a wail of celebration.

Camp Brook Road Comparison: Eleven days can make a world of difference. The top photo of Camp Brook Road was taken on September 6, nine days after the flood. The image below is taken from the same position, eight days later, on September 17.

We Want Stories!
Vermont Folklife Center Seeks Tales of Irene,

October 27

M. D. Drysdale

The Vermont Folklife Center wants to hear your stories of Irene.

The Center will host a series of public meetings and workshops at the Stockbridge Central School to brainstorm ideas for documenting and sharing the personal and community stories of Tropical Storm Irene, its aftermath, and the community response.

The Folklife Center hopes to bring together people from throughout the White River Valley who are interested in documentation projects about the experience of Hurricane Irene.

We envision this as an opportunity for community members to draw inspiration from others by sharing their ideas, work and vision. Together we can explore possibilities for collaboration—between towns, individuals, institutions and community organizations," said spokesperson Aylie Baker.

The Vermont Folklife Center is available at no charge "to partner with individuals and community groups in the White River Valley to offer mentorship for people as they begin projects of their own design."

Baker noted that a Stockbridge resident has already contacted the Center to suggest the idea.

The Stockbridge Historical Society has only one first-hand account of the legendary 1927 Flood, it was noted.

"We were glad she called," notes VFC Executive Director Brent Bjorkman. "We realized that we could offer our expertise in helping communities initiate and execute locally-organized storytelling projects. We strongly believe that these projects have the opportunity to serve hard-hit communities in the present moment as they come together to rebuild."

AFTERWORD

On the eve of Thanksgiving, up to a foot of snow is dumped on the North Country. Then, on our road (Gilead Brook Road) the power goes out around 1 p.m. Despite the obvious contrasts, it is impossible not to harken back to Irene.

Why didn't we buy that generator? What idiots we are!

Back then, we were ensconced in summer; now, we are on the precipice of winter.

Then, the world was green; today, the world is white.

Then, our community was intact; now, our community is scarred, but stronger.

Then, we hadn't done the common sense things one should do to protect themselves from nature's wrath; now, we have failed to take the exact same precautions.

Then, we assumed that the rain and power outage would be a short-lived inconvenience; now, we know differently.

Some people in the area still report that they experience fear when they see or hear rain. Some flinch when they hear the warning beeps from construction equipment. We're mostly healed, but we'll never be the same.

There are no isolated towns and communities at the moment. Most roads and bridges have been fixed. The brooks and rivers, however, still look eerily weird. The once-overgrown banks are now gravel beaches. Boulders have been strategically placed to provide fish habitat, making parts of the stream look like Oriental rock gardens.

A great controversy has arisen between environmentalists and town officials on whether or not it was wise to remove so much gravel from the streams. God knows the state of the fish. You should let the river take its natural course, say the environmentalists. This never would have happened if you had let us remove gravel from the streams like we used to, respond the heavy equipment operators.

It's a debate that will not be resolved before the next flood.

The Thanksgiving issue of *The Herald* was our cut-off for this book. Some of the stories are now complete. The milk trucks can reach the farms. Baseball royalty has come and gone from Vermont Technical College. The roads are mostly plowable. The Bethel sports teams were actually able to finish their seasons (something beyond comprehension to anyone who saw their silt-covered field on August 29).

Many stories are ongoing. The heavy equipment rumbles by our house regularly to remind us that there is work to be done for a long time. The power stays off for four hours, long enough to worry about losing the food in the freezer and to wonder how to cook a turkey in an electric oven. Why didn't we buy a generator? Why didn't we fill the bathtubs with water? Where is our supply of extra batteries? Why didn't we learn our lessons?

Then the power returns. We give thanks, not just for power, but for the holiday, and the return to normalcy. With the covering of snow, you can no longer see the silt on the fields. The river and stream banks no longer look like gravel pits. For the first time since late summer, Vermont looks like Vermont. And for that we are thankful.

Stephen Morris and Sandy Levesque,
Co-Editors

Bethel Gilead Brook Road restoration, November 2011.

We're mostly healed, but we'll never be the same.

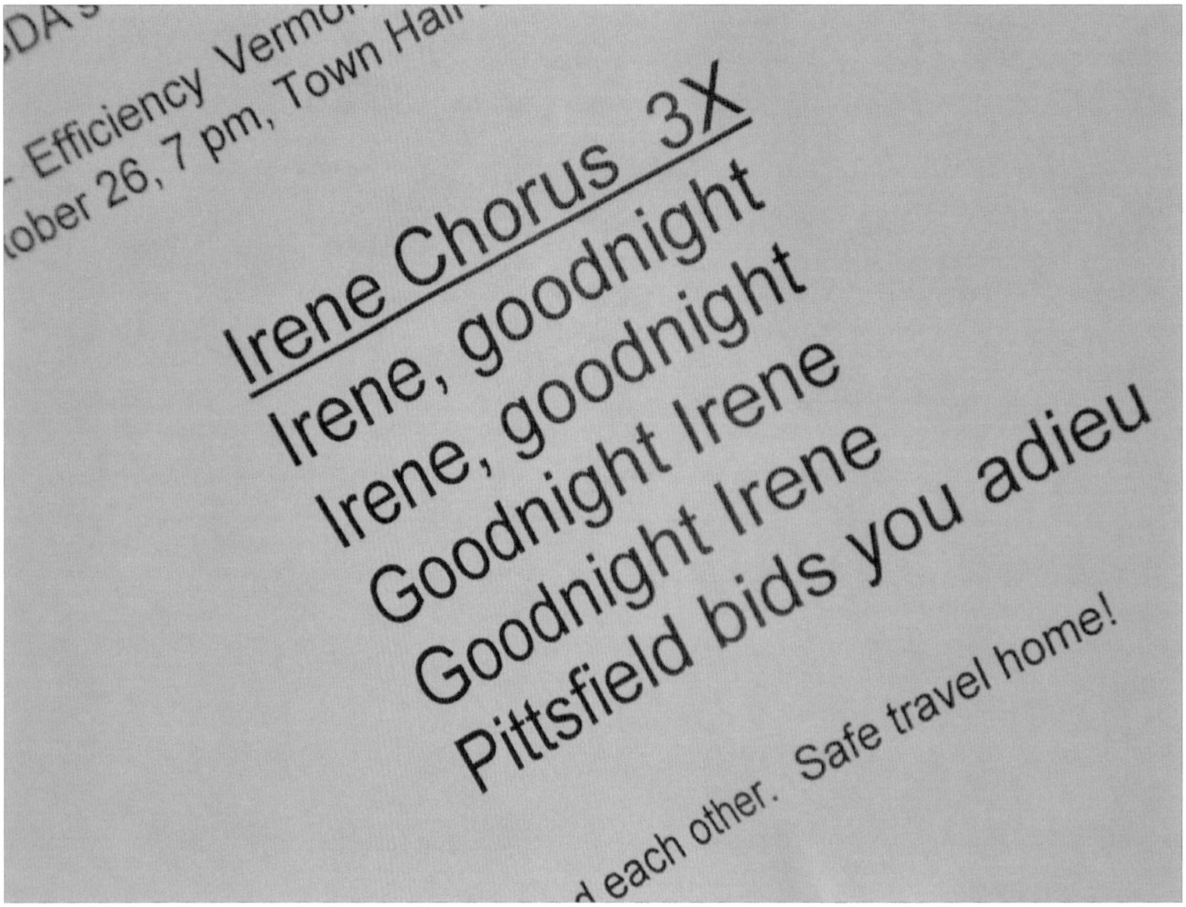

SDA's

- Efficiency Vermo...
October 26, 7 pm, Town Hall...

Irene Chorus 3X

Irene, goodnight
Irene, goodnight
Goodnight Irene
Goodnight Irene
Pittsfield bids you adieu

...d each other. Safe travel home!

Eileen Godfrey of Pittsfield gratefully acknowledges the Maine National Guardsmen as they leave the White River Valley.

CONTRIBUTORS

Scott Beavers has worked in the software industry for the past 15 years and is also the Tunbridge correspondent for *The Herald*. He was unaware of what was happening in the White River Valley when Hurricane Irene hit, but was speechless when he later saw the devastation in South Royalton. He spent the following days helping at a farm in Royalton and residences in South Royalton.

Tim Calabro has been documenting the goings on of the White River Valley in the pages of *The Herald* since 2001. He grew up in South Royalton and now, along with his wife Katie, a mutt named Shay, and two angry cats, calls Randolph his home.

Rebbie Carleton lives in Bethel and teaches art at the Randolph Elementary School, where she was preparing her classroom for the new year on a rainy Sunday afternoon, August 28. When another teacher told her that the River Street Bridge leading to her home was going to be closed, she immediately left for Bethel. By the time she arrived River Street Bridge and all the bridges south of it as far as White River Junction were closed to traffic. Rebbie spent the night in Randolph.

Nancy Cassidy is a graphic designer, photographer and artist. She has been the Composition Supervisor for *The Herald of Randolph* for many years. She lives in Randolph with her husband Chuck. On Monday, August 29, she received a phone call from her granddaughter, Amanda, who was hiking out with her family from their Brink Hill home to Camp Brook Corner after their driveway washed away from flood waters and their generator exploded. Nancy drove through six inches of mud on Route 12 to meet her family and bring them "home."

Shawn Cassidy grew up in Bethel and continues to make his home on Brink Hill with his wife Stephanie and their children, Amanda (16) and Justin (13). In addition to his "day job," Shawn manages Moonlight Motorsports and Vinyl Signs and Graphics. Luckily, Shawn's knowledge of snowmobile trails helped him evacuate his family when the roads were so washed out that even a four-wheeler could not negotiate a path to "civilization."

Laura Craft is the *Herald's* correspondent for Vershire. She lives near the Pompanoosuc River but was fortunate to not experience the full wrath of Irene. Along with her daughter Alice, Laura accompanied her husband and Vershire's Town Clerk, Gene, on a driving tour of the area to document damage for FEEMA.

Central Vermont Public Service provided the courtesy aerial photo of Rochester village.

Amy Danley-White is *The Herald* correspondent for the town of Bethel. Although she doesn't live near the river, she experienced two feet of groundwater flooding her basement during Irene.

Ben DeFlorio, who lives in Randolph with his wife and daughter, is a free-lance photographer, construction consultant, and designer. He is a frequent *Herald* contributor.

Kevin Doering is a public school teacher and trained meteorologist who writes a weekly weather column for *The Herald*. He lives in Randolph Center where, during the storm, he relayed live meteorological information to WDEV in Waterbury and to the National Weather Service in Burlington. Later, he and his two children, Geoffrey and Elissa, helped Vermonters clean out homes and businesses in Rochester, Bethel and Randolph.

M. Dickey Drysdale has been editor and publisher of *The Herald* since 1971. He lives on Braintree Hill and spent the afternoon of the flood unduly worried about the trickle that was running by his house, unaware of the havoc being wreaked elsewhere.

CONTRIBUTORS

Marjorie Drysdale, the wife of *The Herald* editor, is a singer, conductor, music teacher, and occasional feature writer. The evening of the storm seemed rather uneventful, but when she and her husband ventured off their hill, they realized that this was a storm of historic proportions.

Bob Eddy lives on Braintree Hill with his wife Kathy. He is a news, portrait, and landscape photographer, and for 25 years has documented life in the White River Valley for *The Herald*. Providing publication images for a diverse clientele, he has managed First Light Studios in Randolph since 1990.

Lisa Manning Floyd is a Vermont native who, in 1982, moved to the Bethel Lympus area where she now lives with her husband and son. She teaches Humanities in Randolph. Although not directly impacted by Tropical Storm Irene, she was astounded at the devastation and heartened by the way people pulled together and made stronger communities in the hurricane's aftermath.

John Freitag has been the *Herald's* Strafford correspondent for 25 years. He is also the Newton School Facilities Manager and the Town Recreation Board Chair. His concerns during Irene were for the Newton School's Tyson Gym, which had some minor flooding, as well as the town's recreation areas. His worries were justified. Murray Field and the adjoining tennis courts were flooded.

Jim Giberti owns The Imagination Company and Imagination Farm with his partner Kristen Smith. Like most who were cut off from civilization with a backhoe or tractor at their disposal, Jim spent the days after the flood trying to make the roads around him passable. Eventually, he gave into his filmmaker side and went off to grab a few scenes of the damage and the relief efforts in the valley.

Heidi Allen Goodrich is a mother of two young boys, a graphic designer, and the Chelsea correspondent to *The Herald*. She considers herself extremely lucky that the only problem she personally encountered during Irene was the loss of power for nearly two days.

Howard Gunter relocated from Jacksonville, Florida to Vermont in 2008 to become pastor of the Pittsfield Federated Church. Since most of the flood destruction in Pittsfield took place south of the parsonage which is located on the village green, he was unaware of the storm's fury until he heard the ominous drone of heavy equipment early Monday morning. Pastor Gunter was instrumental in establishing the Pittsfield Hurricane Relief Fund, which has raised over $100,000 for the town's flood victims.

Josey Hastings, a teacher and *Herald* contributor, lives high up in the Brookfield hills. She spent the day after Irene in a warehouse in downtown Randolph helping her family throw away boxes upon boxes of flooded caramel, produced on their farm and awaiting shipment.

Tom Hill, a writer and musician, was driven from his home on Davis Hill Road in Stockbridge when all access was destroyed by Hurricane Irene. He now lives in Randolph Center. His column, *Half a Bubble off Plumb*, is published monthly in *The Herald*.

Brent Kay is superintendant of schools in the Randolph area. He submitted the photo of the swamped school buses.

Jerry LeBlond is a professional photographer from Killington, Vermont.

Candace Leslie is a resident of Bryan, Texas whose sister, Suzanne Massonneau, has owned an old house about a mile from Pittsfield village since 1977. Both Candace and Suzanne continue to visit Pittsfield regularly. This year they arrived late in August, little knowing what awaited them.

CONTRIBUTORS

Pamela and Stuart Levasseur are *Herald* correspondents for South Royalton. They live between Route 14 and the White River and spent the night of the hurricane eyeing the southerly end of the street, where rising water was threatening a home. "I have this overwhelming feeling that we had a guardian angel watch over us that night," says Pam.

Sandy Levesque is a marketing consultant, writer, and long time resident of Bethel Gilead Brook Road. The steady thunder of colliding rocks and boulders drew her outside at the height of the storm. She and her husband followed the brook-turned-river until the road washed out and they could no longer watch the trees go down.

Dorothy Manning, the Bethel Lympus correspondent for *The Herald,* has lived in Bethel since 1982. She and her husband, Allen Manning Jr., were stranded in Lympus for nearly a week after Tropical Storm Irene.

Emily Marshia is fortunate to live high on Chelsea's West Hill with her husband, Kevin, their four children, and an array of animals. Her passions include writing, community service, and an aspiration to make her childhood home an active farm again someday.

Jeff Mather lives just above the Rochester flood plain in Rochester village and was able to photograph much of the storm as it occurred, as well as in the weeks to come. His photographs can be seen on his website, www.jeffreymather.com.

Stephen Morris is an editor, publisher, and *Herald* contributor who lives on one of the higher sections of Gilead Brook Road. He spent the night following Irene shoveling water from his basement, but unaware of the devastation and destruction that neighbors on either side of him had suffered.

Zach Nelson is an Ohio University senior majoring in photojournalism. He got his start in 2006 making pictures for *The Herald* where he later spent many summer and winter breaks. Zach happened to arrive in Vermont late the night Irene swept through the state. He spent the following days photographing the hurricane's aftermath.

Kevin Paquet and Cara Louise Tucker of Bethel announced their engagement on Saturday, August 27, under the leading edge of Hurricane Irene. They took the engagement photo the next day on the remains of Bethel's washed-out Findley Bridge.

Cameron Pattison is a student at The Sharon Academy who makes his home in the White River Valley. With a great love for photography, Cameron is a frequent contributor to *The Herald.*

Susan Pelletier is a Lister for the town of Stockbridge. She and her husband, Mark, run a plumbing and heating business in town. Both were heavily involved in the recovery efforts after the storm. (Susan is a former town correspondent for *The Herald.*)

Tom Perera is a retired professor of neuroscience who lives on a hillside in Hancock. Although not directly affected by the flood, he volunteered to assist those who sustained flood damage, especially at Camp Killooleet.

Janet Roberts is "the face at the front desk" at *The Herald*. Hired originally in 1985, she has held positions in accounts receivable, payables, composition, and circulation. She is a lifelong resident of Randolph, married to Keith Mosher, and the mother of two grown sons, Zeb and Zac Chamberlin. She proofread the manuscript for this book and caught a zillion errors before it was sent to press.

CONTRIBUTORS

Jim Robinson is an artist who lives in Bethel and teaches fine art digital imaging at three local colleges. At 12:30 p.m. on August 28, torrents of water created by clogged catch basins and culverts uphill from his house on North Road, entered the basement of his house in three areas. After two frenetic hours and help from his neighbors (one of whom had some sandbags), the rushing waters were diverted from further entering his basement and undermining the foundation.

Kathy Rohloff, a monthly columnist for *The Herald*, lives on the North Road in Bethel. Many of her neighbors suffered devastating losses, but the flood damage ceased just two doors away from her home.

Ginny Sedgewick and her husband Rob were isolated on "Rochester Island" when the Route 73 bridge on one side of their house collapsed under floodwater and the road on the other side turned into a chasm. They used the last of their fuel to fly their powered parachute over Rochester and take photos of the devastation to share with their neighbors. The day after the storm, Ginny drove tourists stranded in the nearby Maple Hill Campground to the top of Great Hawk Road to call their families.

Faye Severy, a fifth- grade teacher in Rochester, lives on Rt. 73 with her husband Frank, a CVPS lineman. Frank reported to the Royalton CVPS office at 8:00 a.m. on Sunday, August 28, and was unable to return home for five days. After the Route 73 bridge was washed out by the flood, Faye crossed the White River for the first time by boat on the morning of August 30. Later that afternoon, townspeople on both sides of the river finished building a footbridge.

Martha Slater is a writer and copy editor for *The Herald*. She lives in the village of Rochester, and was unable to get to work in Randolph for over two weeks after the flood. Her home was undamaged, but many of her neighbors were not so lucky.

Shannon Trigos of Randolph Center understands the importance of reaching out to people in need after spending three years in Columbia as a missionary. On the day of the flood, she watched the devastation unfold on Facebook, but was not prepared to cross Bethel's River Steet Bridge the next morning and find the total loss of Mike and Leslile Piela's home. She helped her long-time friends sort through their few remaining belongings and sent a moving account of the experience to *The Herald*.

Sandy Vondrasek, associate editor of *The Herald*, lives on East Braintree's Peth Road, which survived the storm largely undamaged. On Monday morning, she packed her computer in a backpack, unsure of how or if she could get to work. Facebook posts reported that Randolph's North Main Street Bridge was out. The bridge was not damaged, nor was *The Herald* office—but there was an overwhelming chaos of information to be found inside.

Barb Wood is a wedding photographer from Pittsfield who is never without her camera. It was only after venturing to the end of her road, where she witnessed a swift water rescue on the afternoon of the flood, that she realized the scope of the storm. In the days that followed, Barb became one of Pittsfield's official documentarians, photographing property damage and capturing the amazing spirit of the small town's residents.

Jeff Young is an architect/contractor from Concord, MA who has a cabin in Granville (that he built). He was there during and after the storm. Although "trapped" like everyone else, it proved to be a great opportunity to meet new people and to make new friends. The Youngs have a pig roast every fall to celebrate the coming of winter. This year it was a benefit event that raised over $2,200 for Granville, Rochester, and other people and places damaged by Irene.

Teo Zagar is a documentary filmmaker and state representative from Barnard, Vermont.

PHOTO CREDITS

Tim Calabro	Front Cover, VIII, 18, 19, 25, 28, 40, 45, 59, 61, 68, 69, 72, 74, 76, 110, 111, 112, 113, 123, 131, 134, 135, 146, 147, 151, 153, 158, 159, 163, 164, 165, 167, 168, 172, 177, 179, 191, 192, 193, 195
Rebbie Carleton	201, 202
Nancy Cassidy	15, 16, 17, 20, 21, 22, 56, 63, 196
Shawn Cassidy	54, 55, 56, 66, 128
Central Vermont Public Service	85
Ben DeFlorio	18, 25, 53
Dick Drysdale	155
Marjorie Drysdale	121, 124, 125
Bob Eddy	VII, 47, 48, 49, 50, 51, 52, 57, 88, 89, 91, 92, 93, 94, 114, 115, 116, 117, 118, 119, 126, 129, 155, 157, 160, 161, 171, 175, 189, 193, 197, 198, Back Cover
John Freitag	75, 136
Jim Giberti	194, 219
Heidi Allen Goodrich	70, 71
Tom Hill	41, 42, 43, 80, 125, 148, 149
Jerry LaBlond	30, 31, 32, 83, 86, 87, 90, 95, 97, 98, 99, 101, 102, 103, 142, 143, 178, 180
Sandy Levesque	62, 200, 207
Pamela Levasseur	73
Jeff Mather	29, 33, 96, 98, 141, 145, 181, 205
Cameron Pattison	18
Zach Nelson	32, 77, 100, 133
Jim Robinson	46, 59, 60, 61, 64, 65, 71, 189, 199
Kathy Roloff	127
Faye Severy	24, 27, 28, 30, 99
Martha Slater	17
Barbara Wood	III, V, 23, 26, 27, 34, 35, 36, 37, 38, 39, 44, 79, 81, 82, 84, 104, 105, 106, 107, 108, 109, 137, 138, 139, 182, 183, 184, 185, 186, 208, 209, Back Cover
Nancy Vadnais	176
Jeff Young	169, Back Cover
Teo Zagar	70, 71

All photos copyright © original photographer.

INDEX OF PEOPLE

INDEX OF PEOPLE

INDEX OF PEOPLE

Sales of *The Wrath of Irene* Benefit
Central Vermont Community Action Council

Poverty impacts everyone – young and old, men and women, families and individuals. When one person or family is helped out of poverty, we strengthen our entire community. It takes action, people working together to make a difference.

Founded in 1965, CVCAC helps people achieve economic sufficiency with dignity through individual and family development. We are part of a nationwide network of community action agencies (CAA) established by the Economic Opportunity Act of 1964 in order to fight America's War on Poverty. Today, there are nearly 1,000 CAAs across the United States located in 98% of our cities and counties. CAAs are a primary source of support for the more than 40 million Americans who are living in poverty in both rural and urban areas.

Over the years, CVCAC has earned a reputation for leadership in education on poverty issues, advocacy on behalf of low-income families, and developing innovative strategies and programs to reduce poverty.

As a 501(c)3 nonprofit agency and Community Development Corporation, we provide a number of programs and services for low to moderate income Vermonters aimed at reducing poverty and creating prosperity. We focus our work on the basic tenets of outreach,

Outreach - providing information, education, support services, and referrals to assist those individuals in greatest need access critical resources.

Empowerment - working with individuals to develop their skills and abilities so that they can speak and act on their own behalf and take control of their economic futures.

Advocacy - promoting programs and policies that provide opportunities for self-reliance and promote equal opportunity for all members of our communities.

Organizing - working with individuals and groups and agencies to identify common problems, establish goals, and take appropriate actions to address important social and community issues.

The core source of funding for CAAs comes from the Community Services Block Grant (CSBG) which channels federal funds through the states to local agencies to fight poverty and promote self-sufficiency. Nationally, CSBG funding accounts for less than 10 percent of CAA funding. We use these federal dollars to build and attract additional investments in their programs from state, local, and private sources. In fact, CVCAC is successful in leveraging an average of $20 for every $1 of CSBG funding.

From CVAC.org

About The Herald

T*he Herald of Randolph* has been the voice of the towns in the beautiful White River Valley of Vermont since its founding in 1874. During that time it has had only four publishers and is considered one of the premiere weekly newspapers in Vermont. *The Herald* has won many awards for news and editorial writing and photography from the Vermont Press Association and the New England Press Association.

The Herald's philosophy is to depict the lives of Central Vermont's wonderfully varied people, to celebrate with them their triumphs and successes and to carefully point out where improvements could be made. Would you like to feel connected to small town life in Central Vermont? Log on to *OurHerald.com* or better yet, subscribe.

The Herald of Randolph was established in 1874 by L.P. Thayer when he purchased the *Green Mountain Herald,* published in Randolph. In fact, Randolph's newspaper can be traced back to 1801, when the *Weekly Wanderer* was published in Randolph Center. *The Green Mountain Aegis* was the first newspaper actually published in West Randolph (now, simply, "Randolph). A competing paper, the *Orange County Eagle* started up in 1865. Its name was changed to the *Green Mountain Herald* in 1873.

The Herald began its regional focus in 1874 when the *Randolph Herald* printed separate editions for several White River Valley towns. This is the date considered to be the founding of *The Herald.* The newspaper was purchased by L.B. Johnson in 1894, and the current offices were built in 1899. In 1941 Johnson changed the name to *The White River Valley Herald.*

John Drysdale bought the paper in 1945 and continued its regional emphasis and independent viewpoint. In 1960 he introduced the offset printing method to *The Herald* making it the first newspaper in Vermont to do so. His son, M. Dickey Drysdale, became publisher in 1973.

The Herald
P.O. Box 309, Randolph, Vermont 05060
(802) 728-3232 FAX (802) 728-9275

The Turks' barn on Bethel's Camp Brook Road.

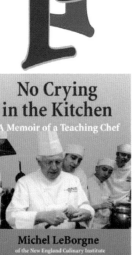
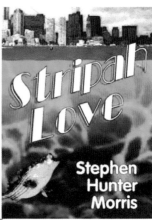

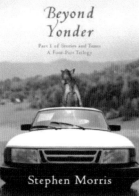
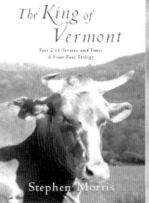

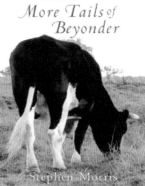

Made in the USA
Charleston, SC
27 March 2012